© 2009 National Center for Competency Testing

NOTICE

This NCCT review book is designed to help certification candidates review material they have previously learned by formal schooling and/or by experience, but it is *not* designed as a textbook. Candidates who find any of this material to be new to them may need to consult with their instructors, mentors, texts, or other references before testing.

The sample test questions in this book will be *typical* of the types of questions on the corresponding exams, and *similar* to them in construction and content, but will not be the same.

The sample case studies in this book will be typical of the types of situations or scenarios that may be found on the job, and reviewing them will help examination candidates use higher level thinking skills that will be required on the examination as well.

RE: ABBREVIATIONS

Medical abbreviations are time savers, but they are subject to misinterpretation and the same word may be abbreviated in more than one way. In addition, abbreviations may be capitalized or in lower case, and written with or without punctuation. Please remember that slight variations are common when studying, reviewing, and taking tests that include abbreviations in them.

COPYRIGHT 2009
© **by the National Center for Competency Testing.**

Reproduction or translation of any part of this work beyond that permitted by Sections 107 or 108 of the 1976 United States Copyright Act without the permission of the copyright owner is unlawful. No part of this work may be reproduced or used in any form or by any means-graphic, electronic, or mechanical, including photocopying, recording, taping, or information storage and retrieval systems without written permission of the publisher.

TABLE OF CONTENTS

PREFACE	**DIRECTIONS** How to Use This Review - 5

PART I	**EXAMINATION CONTENT** Test Item Grid – 7 Expanded Content Outline - 9

PART II	**REVIEW QUESTIONS**
	I. Medical Office Management -13
	    A. Law and Ethics -13
	    B. Communication, Equipment and Supplies -23
	    C. Financial Management -27
	
	II. Medical Terminology -37
	    A. Foundations of Word Structure
	    B. Abbreviations
	
	III. Pharmacology -47
	    Administration of Medication
	
	IV. Anatomy and Physiology -55
	
	V. Medical Procedures -77
	    A. Infection Control, Exposure Control, and Safety -77
	    B. Patient Examination and Clinical Skills -85
	    C. Phlebotomy -93
	    D. Diagnostic Testing and Lab Procedures (combined with C.)
	        Basic Lab Skills and Respiratory Training -93
	        Electrocardiography -101

	REFERENCES - 111

PART III	**CASE APPLICATIONS** Case (1) Medical Office Management (Law & Ethics) -113 Case (2) Medical Office Management (Communication & Equipment/Supplies) -114 Case (3) Medical Office Management (Financial Management) -115 Case (4) Medical Terminology -117 Case (5) Anatomy and Physiology -119 Case (6) Medical Procedures (Infection & Exposure Control) -120 Case (7) Medical Procedures (Patient Exam & Clinical Skills) -120 Case (8) Medical Procedures (Phlebotomy) -122 Case (9) Pharmacology - 123 Case (10) Diagnostic Testing and Procedures (Lab)-124

ANSWER KEY - 127

I. Medical Office Management - 127
    A. Law and Ethics -127
    B. Communication, Equipment and Supplies -128
    C. Financial Management -129

II. Medical Terminology -130
    A. Foundations of Word Structure
    B. Abbreviations

III. Pharmacology -131

IV. Anatomy and Physiology -132

V. Medical Procedures -135
    A. Infection Control, Exposure Control, and Safety -135
    B. Patient Examination and Clinical Skills -136
    C. Phlebotomy -137
    D. Diagnostic Testing and Lab Procedures (combined with C.)
        Basic Lab Skills and Respiratory Training
        Electrocardiography -138

ANSWERS TO CASES -140

Case (1) Medical Office Management (Law & Ethics) -140
Case (2) Medical Office Management (Communication & Equipment/Supplies) -141
Case (3) Medical Office Management (Financial Management) -144
Case (4) Medical Terminology -145
Case (5) Anatomy and Physiology -146
Case (6) Medical Procedures (Infection & Exposure Control) -146
Case (7) Medical Procedures (Patient Exam & Clinical Skills) -147
Case (8) Medical Procedures (Phlebotomy) -149
Case (9) Pharmacology - 150
Case (10) Diagnostic Testing and Procedures (Lab)-151

NCCT Certification Exam Review
HOW to USE this REVIEW

Part I. Examination Content provides a content grid related to the competencies that are expected of a practitioner at entry level. These competencies define the role being certified, and have been substantiated by experts in the field. The actual certification exam is designed using a Content Grid that was built from these competencies. Use the grid to predict where your strengths and weaknesses in preparation may lie, and use your textbook to review sections before moving to Part II.

Part II. Review and Reference provides review practice questions that can be self-scored. The best way to use this part of the Review Book is to answer the questions fully (on paper is best) *before* looking at the answer key. That makes this review about "testing yourself" rather than "learning as you go." In addition, there will be a listing of references at the end of this section if you need more study.

Part III. Case Application provides a section with simulated cases or scenarios designed to make you exercise critical thinking skills by making decisions and solving problems using a reality-based reality based review. If you have trouble with these cases, you may need more practical experience or study time so that you can apply what you have learned.

Part I. Examination Content

Part I. Examination Content provides a Content Grid that explains the competencies that are expected of a practitioner at entry level. These competencies define the role being certified, and have been substantiated by experts in the field. The actual certification exam is designed using this Content Grid. Use the grid to guide how much time you should expect to spend in preparation for each topic category, and use your textbook to review sections before moving to Part II.

Topics	% Test Content
Medical Office Management (MO)	18 - 20.5% (8% = Insurance & Bookkeeping)
Medical Terminology (MT)	10-12.5%
Pharmacology (PH)	10-12.5%
Anatomy & Physiology (AN)	10-12.5%

Medical Procedures (MP)
    Phlebotomy
    Patient Examination
    ECG / other lab
    Infection and Exposure Control
	
	 10-12.5%
	 10-12.5%
	 10-12.5%
	 12.5%

TOTAL	100%

*See detailed content outline on page 9

The NCCT Medical Assistant (NCMA) Examination may have test items that are written at any of *three levels*, as certification testing requires more than merely knowing facts. It requires the use of higher level thinking skills as well. Keep that in mind when looking over the material.

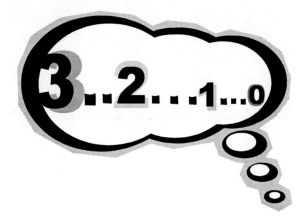

- **Low level**—asks the examinee to recall a fact or remember information previously learned. (For example: An evacuated phlebotomy tube with what color top is usually drawn for a CBC?) Most of the examination questions are written at this level.

- **Middle level**—asks the examinee to interpret or apply information in answering a question. (For example: What precaution in post puncture care would be appropriate for a patient with hemophilia?) Some examination questions are written at this level.

- **High level**—asks the examinee to solve a problem or make a decision. (For example: If a red top tube must be drawn and there are no red top tubes left, can any other tube be substituted?) A few examination questions are written at this level.

If you have questions about material or answers you don't understand after checking with your textbook or your instructor, we can refer your questions to our consultants if you use the "Contact Us" function at our website: www.ncctinc.com . Our customer service telephone staff cannot answer content questions, as the people who write the reviews are subject matter experts who are consultants with NCCT. They do not work here on a full time basis. In your written communication, please include:

(1) Your name
(2) Your email address
(3) Your question about the content
(4) The page # to which you are referring
(and the question # if it's a test question)
(5) Your supporting documentation (i.e. name of a textbook, author, edition, and page number) to which we can refer

By sending email, we will have a written electronic record of your question to forward to the experts, and a method for follow-up to be sure we not only address any changes that need to be made for the next edition, but can reply to you directly.

Medical Assisant Certification Exam Content Outline
National Center for Competency Testing ®
7007 College Boulevard, Suite 705
Overland Park, KS 66211 www.ncctinc.com
Phone 800-875-4404; Fax 913-498-1243
Office Hours M-F 8:30am-5:00pm CST

Approximate % of Exam	Content Categories
10-12.5%	**Anatomy and Physiology**
	• Body Systems and Functions
	• Basic Disease Recognition
	• Bones
	• Body Positioning for examination
	• Major muscles
18-20.5%	**Medical Office Management**
	• General Office Management Duties (10-12.5% of exam)
	1. Oral and written communication skills
	2. Legal concepts
	3. Patient instruction
	4. Computers
	5. Equipment operation and maintenance
	6. Organizational skills
	7. Cultural awareness
	8. Medical record keeping
	• Bookkeeping (4% of exam)
	1. Basic banking
	2. Basic accounting
	3. Record keeping
	4. Preparing and collecting patient accounts
	5. Payroll
	• Insurance Processing (4% of exam)
	1. Managed care models
	2. Insurance plans
	3. Referrals and precertification
	4. Filing claims
	5. Third party payers
	6. Basic procedural and diagnostic coding for reimbursement; DRGs
	Medical Procedures
	(including understanding Scope of Practice in all areas of medical procedures)
12.5%	• Infection and Exposure Control
	1. Biohazardous waste disposal
	2. Exposure control
	3. Asepsis
	4. Personal Protective Equipment
	5. Universal Precautions: blood and body fluids
	6. Sanitation, sterilization, and disinfection
	7. OSHA safety regulations
10-12.5%	• Patient Examination and Clinical Skills

	1. Patient history and screening; charting
	2. Basic patient examination skills: vitals; temperature; other measurements
	3. Assistance in minor surgical procedures
	4. Bandaging or dressing wounds; suture/staple removal
	5. Assistance with therapeutic modalities
	6. Vision testing (e.g. acuity; color blindness)
	7. Specialty testing (e.g. allergy)
	8. Recognition of normal and abnormal conditions
	9. Patient instruction
	10. Comprehension of scope of practice (including state law)
10-12.5%	• Phlebotomy
	1. Venipuncture and capillary puncture
	2. Patient preparation and site selection/prep
	3. Safety and infection control; QC
	4. Equipment & tubes (types, uses, limitations, additives, collection amounts)
	5. Coagulation and anticoagulation
10-12.5%	• ECG and other Diagnostic Testing and Lab Procedures
	1. CLIA waived lab testing, including QC
	2. Specimen collection (e.g. urine, throat, stool, wound, etc.)
	3. ECG (12 lead) testing, monitoring, troubleshooting
	4. Basic respiratory testing
10-12.5%	**Medical Terminology**
	• Foundations of word structure (roots, prefixes, suffixes)
	• Standard medical / pharmaceutical abbreviations and symbols
	• Terms re: Insurance Processing, Anatomy & Physiology, Law, Ethics
	• Terms re: Surgical Procedures, Common Diseases, Common Pathology
10-12.5%	**Pharmacology**
	• Use of Pharmaceutical Desk References (e.g. PDR and others)
	• Basic drug calculations and metric conversions
	• Pharmacology terms and abbreviations
	• Legal prescription requirements for all drug schedules and classes
	• Common drugs and their classifications/side effects /indications for use
	• DEA regulations
	• Safe preparation and administration of medications (e.g. oral, topical, subcutaneous, intramuscular) and other routes
100%	**Total**

Part II. Review and Reference

Part II. Review and Reference provides summary information and/or practice questions that can be self-scored. The best way to use this part of the exam is to answer the questions fully BEFORE looking at the answer key. That makes this review about "testing yourself" rather than "learning as you go." In addition, there will be a listing of references in this section if you need more study.

PREFACE: PLEASE READ CAREFULLY

The purpose of this examination review book is to enable Medical Assistants to become better educated and knowledgeable in their allied health field and to become prepared for the National Center for Competency Testing certification examination.

The questions contained herein are in multiple-choice form and may be similar to those found in the NCCT certification examination, but this review book is *not constructed to provide the exact questions* found on any one specific exam version. Likewise, there is no guarantee that purchase or study of this review material will result automatically in a passing grade. Passing the exam is a function of each individual's training, level of learning, experience, preparation, and personal ability.

Due to the ever-changing procedures and knowledge in the every profession, there may occasionally be inaccuracies and ambiguities in a review question ; therefore, we suggest that when in doubt about any information during review, you should check your own resource material. Customer service representatives at NCCT will not be able to answer questions about review or test content, as review materials are written and revised by consultants who are not available at the NCCT offices to answer questions. We recommend you consult your textbooks and instructors if in question on anything before the exam. If you believe there is an error in the manual, feel free to alert us to it by email through the website at www.ncctinc.com.

Our desire is that this review book will be a stepping-stone to new knowledge, appreciation, and advancement in the allied health field.

I. Medical Office Management
A. Law & Ethics

Review Questions

1. Right and wrong conduct is known as _____.

   a. empathy
   b. criminal law
   c. ethics
   d. licensure

2. The most common type of medical tort liability is _____.

   a. negligence
   b. breach of contract
   c. breach of confidence
   d. fraud and deceit

3. A person being sued is called the _____.

   a. plaintiff
   b. tort
   c. defendant
   d. criminal law

4. The withdrawal of a physician from the care of a patient without reasonable notice of such discharge from the case by the patient is _____.

   a. contract
   b. reasonable care
   c. negligence
   d. abandonment

5. An unlawful threat or attempt to do bodily injury to another is _____.

   a. litigation
   b. assault
   c. crime
   d. libel

6. The health worker is protected by law if it can be determined that he or she acted reasonable as compared with fellow workers. This is called _____.

   a. respondeat superior
   b. reasonable care
   c. duty of care
   d. statute

7. Negligence by a professional person is called _____.

   a. invasion of privacy
   b. slander
   c. malpractice
   d. tort

8. An act that violates criminal law is called _____.

   a. defamation
   b. crime
   c. libel
   d. slander

9. The breaking of a law, promise, or duty is called _____.

   a. statute
   b. breach
   c. consent
   d. incompetent

10. The ability to see things from another person's point of view is _____.

    a. consent
    b. respondeat superior
    c. empathy
    d. ethics

11. The time established for filing law suits is _____.

    a. civil law
    b. statute of limitations
    c. contract
    d. no correct answer

12. A writ that commands a witness to appear at a trial or other proceeding and to give testimony is a(n) _____.

    a. habeas corpus
    b. tort of appearance
    c. subpoena
    d. tort et a travers

13. A wrong committed against another person or the person's property is a _____.

    a. defamation
    b. libel
    c. tort
    d. plaintiff

14. Holding or detaining a person against his will is _____.

    a. false imprisonment
    b. crime
    c. incompetent
    d. duty of care

15. A violation of a person's right not to have his or her name, photograph, or private affairs exposed of made public without giving consent is _____.

    a. false imprisonment
    b. malpractice
    c. invasion of privacy
    d. statute

16. A major crime for which greater punishment is imposed other than a misdemeanor is _____.

    a. licensure
    b. civil law
    c. tort
    d. felony

17. One who institutes a lawsuit is _____.

    a. defendant
    b. plaintiff
    c. litigation
    d. respondeat superior

18. A legal statement of how an individual's property is to be distributed after death is _____.

    a. contract
    b. tort
    c. will
    d. judgment

19. Information given by a patient to medical personnel which cannot be disclosed without consent of the person who gave it is _____.

    a. duty of care
    b. respondeat superior
    c. judgment
    d. privileged communication

20. A rule of conduct made by a government body is _____.

    a. tort
    b. law
    c. will
    d. contract

21. Failure to do something that a reasonable person would do under ordinary circumstances that ends up causing harm to another person or a person's property is _____.

    a. malpractice
    b. negligence
    c. slander
    d. defamation

22. Permission granted by a person voluntarily and in his right mind is _____.

    a. consent
    b. litigation
    c. breach
    d. duty of care

23. Injuring the name and reputation of another person by making false statements to a third person is _____.

    a. empathy
    b. negligence
    c. defamation
    d. ethics

24. An agreement between two or more parties for the doing or not doing of some definite thing is _____.

    a. contract
    b. litigation
    c. statute
    d. felony

25. Lack of physical or mental fitness is known as _____.

    a. breach of duty
    b. abandonment
    c. competence
    d. incompetence

26. The final decision of a court in an action or suit is _____.

    a. consent
    b. contract
    c. judgment
    d. licensure

27. Responsibility of an employer for the acts of an employee is _____.

    a. libel
    b. malpractice
    c. respondeat superior
    d. civil law

28. A Latin term signifying that a person is not of sound mind is _____.

    a. res gestae
    b. non compos mentis
    c. res judicata
    d. tecum

29. A person who is no longer under the care, custody, or supervision of a parent is called a(n) _____.

    a. emancipated minor
    b. plaintiff
    c. defendant
    d. tort

30. An impartial panel established to listen to and investigate patient's complaints about medical care or excessive fees is called a _____ committee.

    a. medical ethics
    b. medical grievance
    c. civil law
    d. no correct answer

31. Latin for "things done; deeds"; the facts and circumstances attendant to the act in question would be called _____.

    a. res gestae
    b. locum tenems
    c. tecum
    d. no correct answer

32. Testimony of a witness under oath and written down before trial for possible use when the case comes to trial is _____.

    a. deposition
    b. citation
    c. warrant
    d. expert testimony

33. A statute that enforces private right and liabilities, as differentiated from criminal law is called a _____.

    a. statute of limitations
    b. civil law
    c. medical arbitration
    d. no correct answer

34. Violation or omission of a legal or moral duty is called _____.

    a. negligence
    b. breach of duty
    c. defamation
    d. malpractice

35. A deliberate physical attack upon a person is called _____.

    a. assault
    b. battery
    c. slander
    d. contributory negligence

36. Latin for "he who acts through another acts for himself" is called _____.

    a. res gestae
    b. qui facit per alium facit per se
    c. locum tenems
    d. no correct answer

37. The branch of study of moral issues, questions, and problems arising in the practice of medicine and in biomedical research is called _____.

    a. bioethics
    b. litigation
    c. philosophy
    d. privileged communication

38. A statement given concerning some scientific, technical, or professional matter by an expert, such as a physician is called _____.

    a. litigation
    b. expert testimony
    c. medical arbitration
    d. burden of proof

39. A *patient's* failure to act prudently and reasonably, or doing that which a reasonable person would not do under similar circumstances is called _____.

    a. breach of duty
    b. assumption of risk
    c. contributory negligence
    d. no correct answer

40. Consent to treatment based on a full understanding of all possible risks of unpreventable results of that treatment is called _____.

    a. contributory negligence
    b. fraud
    c. assumption of risk
    d. proximate cause

41. Conduct, courtesy, and manners that are customarily used in a medical office by medical professionals are known as _____.

    a. ethics
    b. moral therapy
    c. precocity
    d. medical etiquette

42. An intentional perversion of truth for the purpose of inducing another in reliance upon it to part with some valuable thing belonging to him or to surrender a legal right is called _____.

    a. fraud
    b. negligence
    c. assumption of risk
    d. contributory negligence

43. To interrupt or discontinue a suit temporarily with the intention or resumption at a later date, or to ask for a continuance is called a _____.

    a. suspension
    b. judgment
    c. civil law
    d. deposition

44. Latin for "things decided"—that is, a matter already decided by judicial authority is called _____.

    a. res judicata
    b. respondeat superior
    c. locum tenems
    d. no correct answer

45. That which in natural and continuous sequence, unbroken by any new independent cause, produces an event, and without which the injury would not have occurred is called _____.

    a. negligence
    b. proximate cause
    c. assumption of risk
    d. assault

46. The presumption or inference of negligence when an accident is otherwise unable to be explained in terms of ordinary and known experience is called _____.

    a. res judicata
    b. res ipsa loquitur
    c. locum tenems
    d. res gestae

47. Failure to achieve an agreed upon result, even when the highest degree of skill has been used, is called _____.

    a. breach of contract
    b. negligence
    c. proximate cause
    d. ethics

48. What license must a physician have to dispense, prescribe or administer controlled substances?

    a. Lawyers
    b. Narcotic
    c. Business
    d. Occupational

49. Unauthorized disclosure of information regarding any patient to a third party may result in _____.

    a. civil law liability
    b. medical liability
    c. invasion of privacy
    d. defamation of character

50. Medical research is often published in medical journals that are evaluated by members of the medical community through a process known as _____.

    a. professional review
    b. hospital review
    c. peer review
    d. promethium review

51. Under the Peer Review Improvement Act of 1982, Peer Review Organizations are responsible for the review for appropriateness and necessity of putting a patient into the hospital by a process known as _____ review.

    a. procedure
    b. admissions
    c. cost
    d. quality

52. A fraudulent signature is called _____.

    a. endorsement
    b. forgery
    c. fraud
    d. forbearance

53. _____ are defined as what are right and wrong.

    a. Rules
    b. Ethics
    c. Laws
    d. Guidelines

54. Which one of the following might involve a decision based upon bioethics?

    a. Reporting physical, emotional or mental abuse
    b. Treating a 16 year old girl who is pregnant without parental consent
    c. The use of fetal tissue transplantation for research
    d. Reporting to the authorities a suicidal patient

55. A physician must have the patient's permission in writing to reveal any confidential information except for which one of the following?

    a. Gunshot wound
    b. Anorexia
    c. Drug addiction
    d. Pregnancy

56. It is _____ to deny treatment to an HIV infected patients.

    a. illegal
    b. moral
    c. unethical
    d. ethical

57. _____ is a federal regulation that requires health care professionals to protect the privacy and confidentiality of patients' health information.

    a. OSHA
    b. CLIA
    c. CMS
    d. HIPAA

58. In the health care field the acronym HIPAA stands for _____.

    a. Health Information Adjustment Association
    b. History Inquiry of Professional Assertive Assistance
    c. Health Insurance Portability and Accountability Act
    d. Health Inquiry for Permission of Accountability Association

59. The statement *"A physician shall respect the law"* is a part of the _____.

    a. AAMA Code of Ethics
    b. AMA Code of Principles
    c. preamble to the constitution of the United States
    d. AMA Code of Ethics

60. Which of these generally results from an act of carelessness, without an intent to harm?

    a. breach of confidentiality
    b. malpractice
    c. slander
    d. manslaughter

I. Medical Office Management
B. Communication, Equipment and Supplies

Review Questions

1. A system whereby large quantities of data can be accessed, searched, sorted, and arranged very rapidly by computer is called a(n) _____ system.

    a. word processing
    b. electronic scheduling
    c. research
    d. database management

2. A computer monitor, hard drive, and printer are known as _____.

    a. software
    b. hardware
    c. processing equipment
    d. visual displays

3. The term for the technology that tells a computer what to do is known as the _____.

    a. ram
    b. software
    c. hardware
    d. disc space

4. The computer key DEL command means _____.

    a. deliver
    b. delete
    c. discard
    d. directory

5. The computer's directional arrow keys _____.

    a. start the machine
    b. are used with the control key
    c. move the cursor, right, left, up or down
    d. correct typing mistakes

6. Referring to computers, the term "user friendly" refers to _____.

   a. how well written the manual is
   b. how many documents the system will handle
   c. can the system be cost effective
   d. how easy the system is to operate

7. The process of changing words into numbers so that computers can be used in processing insurance claims is called _____.

   a. coding
   b. word manipulation
   c. classification
   d. diagnostic numbering

8. A business letter written in full block style will have all lines _____.

   a. right justified
   b. indented 5 spaces
   c. equally spaced vertically
   d. at the left hand margin

9. Making a duplicate file to protect computer information from being lost is called making a _____.

   a. backup
   b. batch
   c. saved disc
   d. copy

10. When writing a business letter, the salutation of a letter should be followed by which punctuation mark?

    a. Comma
    b. None
    c. Asterisk
    d. Colon

11. A newsletter that weighs less than one pound would be considered _____ class mail.

    a. first
    b. second
    c. third
    d. fourth

12. What office instrument is designed to receive and send printed documents via the telephone?

    a. Wire service
    b. Office scanner
    c. Fax machine
    d. Copy machine

13. Business or handwritten mail that weighs less than 11 ounces is known as _____ class mail.

    a. first
    b. second
    c. third
    d. fourth

14. Parcel post or _____ class mail is used for bound printed matter, film, & sound recordings.

    a. first
    b. second
    c. third
    d. fourth

15. Before placing a telephone caller on hold it is appropriate to _____.

    a. ask if you may put the caller on hold
    b. wait for the caller to confirm they can wait
    c. obtain a return phone number
    d. all answers are correct

16. An incoming call should be answered by the _____ ring.

    a. first
    b. second
    c. third
    d. fourth

17. Which one of the following items is **not** needed when taking a routine phone message?

    a. Caller's name
    b. Caller's return phone number
    c. Current days date
    d. Caller's drivers license #

18. Prior to answering an incoming call the medical assistant should _____.

    a. smile
    b. finish up with previous call
    c. screen the call with caller ID
    d. release any anger

19. When handling incoming mail the medical assistant should _____.

    a. initial each piece of opened mail
    b. open only mail marked "personal"
    c. attach the envelope to the correspondence
    d. all answers are correct

20. A letter should be folded in _____ using a #10 envelope?

    a. half horizontally
    b. half vertically
    c. thirds face-up
    d. fourths face-down

21. _____ is the study of words and their relationship to other words in a sentence.

    a. Etiquette
    b. Forum
    c. Punctuation
    d. Grammar

22. When handling a patient complaint which one of the following would be most appropriate?

    a. If the patient is angry, match his/her anger level, and s/he will calm down
    b. Take all complaints seriously and take thorough notes
    c. Refuse to talk to patients who are complaining; the doctor should handle them
    d. No correct answer

23. When working with patients from a culture different than your own, one should _____.

    a. encourage them to speak English
    b. show respect for their culture
    c. speak loudly so they will understand
    d. refrain from making eye contact

24. Body language, body posture, space and distance are all examples of _____.

    a. non-verbal communication
    b. verbal communication
    c. written communication
    d. all answers are correct

25. When caring for patients with physical disabilities, which of these is not an appropriate consideration for most?

    a. Do not rush them
    b. Ask if they need assistance before giving assistance
    c. Provide ample space for patients using assistive devices for mobility
    d. Speak loudly

I. Medical Office Management
C. Financial Management

Review Questions

1. A bed patient in a hospital is called a(n) _____.

   a. inpatient
   b. outpatient
   c. third party payer
   d. provider

2. A person who represents either party of an insurance claim is the _____.

   a. doctor
   b. adjuster
   c. provider
   d. subscriber

3. A request for payment under an insurance contractor bond is called a(n) _____.

   a. insurance application
   b. claim
   c. dual choice request
   d. total disability

4. Payment made periodically to keep an insurance policy in force is called _____.

   a. time limit
   b. premium
   c. coinsurance
   d. fee-for-service

5. A person or institution that gives medical care is a(n) _____.

   a. third-party payer
   b. provider
   c. adjuster
   d. insurance agent

6. Benefits that are made in the form of cash payments are known as _____.

   a. indemnities
   b. deductibles
   c. medical co-pays
   d. cash advances

27

7. An amount the insured must pay before policy benefits begin is called _____.

   a. indemnity
   b. extended benefits
   c. deductible
   d. catastrophic

8. An organization that offers health insurance at a fixed monthly premium with little or no deductible and works through a primary care provider is called a(n)_____.

   a. preferred provider
   b. health maintenance organization
   c. member physician
   d. private health provider

9. Health insurance that provides protection against the high cost of treating severe or lengthy illnesses or disabilities is called _____.

   a. catastrophic
   b. severe
   c. third-party payer
   d. no correct answer

10. A patient receiving ambulatory care at a hospital or other health facility without being admitted as a bed patient is called a(n) _____.

    a. inpatient
    b. outpatient
    c. carrier
    d. adjuster

11. An injury that prevents a worker from performing one or more of the regular functions of his job would be known as a _____.

    a. partial disability
    b. permanent disability
    c. total disability
    d. resultant disability

12. A previous injury, disease or physical condition that existed before the health insurance policy was issued is called _____.

    a. preexisting condition
    b. prior exposure
    c. foregoing condition
    d. no correct answer

13. One who belongs to a group insurance plan is called _____.

    a. third-party payer
    b. subscriber
    c. carrier
    d. no correct answer

14. A sum of money provided in an insurance policy, payable for covered services is called _____.

    a. deductible
    b. benefits
    c. dues payable
    d. premium

15. To prevent the insured from receiving a duplicate payment for losses under more than one insurance policy is called _____.

    a. fee-for-service
    b. hospital benefits
    c. coordination of benefits
    d. non duplication benefits

16. When a patient has health insurance, the percentage of covered services that is the responsibility of the patient to pay is known as _____.

    a. coinsurance
    b. pre-defined policy
    c. comprehensive
    d. in percent policy

17. Insurance that is meant to offset medical expenses resulting from a catastrophic illness is called _____.

    a. primary insurance
    b. major medical
    c. whole life policy
    d. comprehensive

18. An unexpected event which may cause injury is called _____.

    a. dread disease rider
    b. accident
    c. adjuster
    d. no correct answer

19. A doctor who agrees to accept an insurance companies pre-established fee as the maximum amount to be collected is called _____.

    a. subscriber
    b. claim representative
    c. participating physician
    d. adjuster

20. Insurance plans that pay a physician's full charge if it does not exceed his normal charge or does not exceed the amount normally charged for the service is called _____.

    a. usual, customary and reasonable
    b. comprehensive
    c. dual choice
    d. no correct answer

21. A notice of insurance claim or proof of loss must be filed within a designated _____ or it can be denied.

    a. waiting period
    b. policy date
    c. time limit
    d. grace period

22. A health program for people age 65 and older under social security is called _____.

    a. Tri-Care
    b. Medicare
    c. Champva
    d. Workers' Compensation

23. A civilian health and medical program of the uniform services is called _____.

    a. Tri-Care
    b. Medicare
    c. Medicaid
    d. Workers' Compensation

24. A form of insurance paid by the employer providing cash benefits to workers injured or disabled in the course of employment is called _____.

    a. Tri-Care
    b. Champus
    c. Workers' Compensation
    d. Medicaid

25. A recap sheet that accompanies a Medicare or Medicaid check, showing breakdown and explanation of payment on a claim is called _____.

    a. fee-for-service
    b. explanation of benefits
    c. coordination of benefits
    d. dual choice

26. A type of insurance whereby the insured pays a specific amount per unit of service and the insurer pays the rest of the cost is called _____.

    a. co-payment
    b. coordination of benefits
    c. deductible
    d. indemnity

27. In insurance, greater coverage of diseases or an accident, and greater indemnity payment in comparison with a limited clause is called _____.

    a. co-payment
    b. comprehensive
    c. deductible
    d. major medical

28. A rider added to a policy to provide additional benefits for certain conditions is called _____.

    a. hospital benefits
    b. dread disease rider
    c. preexisting condition
    d. no correct answer

29. An interval after a payment is due to the insurance company in which the policy holder may make payments, and still the policy remains in effect is called _____.

    a. extended benefits
    b. grace period
    c. coordination of benefits
    d. lapse time

30. An agreement by which a patient assigns to another party the right to receive payment from a third party for the service the patient has received is called _____.

    a. assignment of benefits
    b. coordination of benefits
    c. non duplication of benefits
    d. no correct answer

31. A skilled nursing facility for patients receiving specialized care after discharge from a hospital is called _____.

    a. extended care facility
    b. post care facility
    c. nursing home
    d. no correct answer

32. Payment for hospital charges incurred by an insured person because of injury or illness is called _____.

    a. hospital benefits
    b. catastrophic health benefits
    c. extra help benefits
    d. no correct answer

33. An agent of an insurance company who solicits or initiates contracts for insurance coverage and services, and is the policyholder for the insurer is called _____.

    a. insurance agent
    b. claim representative
    c. carrier
    d. member physician

34. A method of charging whereby a physician presents a bill for each service rendered is called _____.

    a. non duplication of benefits
    b. fee-for-service
    c. monthly statement
    d. no correct answer

35. The Tri-Care fiscal year is from _____.

    a. January 1 to December 31
    b. October 1 to September 1
    c. October 1 to September 30
    d. July 1 to June 31

36. The number on the Employees Withholding Exemption Certificate is _____.

    a. W-2
    b. W-4
    c. 1040
    d. W-3

37. FICA provides benefits for _____.

    a. Medicare
    b. social security
    c. old age
    d. aid to dependent children

38. As part of the office bookkeeping procedures, the physician's bank statement should be reconciled with the _____.

    a. daily ledger
    b. business ledger
    c. personal ledger
    d. checkbook

39. A record of debits, credits, and balances is referred to as a patient's _____.

    a. sheet
    b. chart
    c. ledger
    d. slip

40. A signature on the reverse side of a check is called _____.

    a. kiting
    b. endorsement
    c. reconciliation
    d. signature card

41. A form to itemize deposits made to savings or checking accounts is called _____.

    a. deposit slip
    b. money order
    c. check guarantee
    d. no correct answer

42. To correct a handwritten error in a patient's chart, it is only acceptable to _____.

    a. white it out neatly and insert the correct information
    b. write over the error
    c. scratch through the error so it cannot be read
    d. draw a line through the error, insert the correct information, date and initial it

43. Low income patients can be covered by what type of insurance?

    a. Medicaid
    b. Medicare
    c. Tri-Care
    d. Blue Cross/Blue Shield

44. The reference procedural code book that uses a numbering system developed by the AMA is called a(n)_____.

    a. reference manual
    b. current procedural terminology
    c. insurance claim manual
    d. manual for current procedures

45. _____ is a method used for determining whether a particular service or procedure is covered under a patient's policy.

    a. Informed consent
    b. Preauthorization
    c. Pre-certification
    d. No correct answer

46. The International Classification of Disease, 9th Revision, Clinical Modification (ICD-9-CM) is used to code _____.

    a. procedures
    b. diagnoses
    c. services rendered
    d. medications

47. In insurance coding using an "E" code designates _____.

    a. a factor that contributes to a condition or disease
    b. classification of environmental events, such as poisoning
    c. the primary diagnosis
    d. cancers

48. E/M codes are located in the _____ manual.

    a. CPT
    b. ICD-9-CM
    c. ICD-10-CM
    d. HCPC

49. Which codes can modifiers be added to, to indicate that a procedure or service has been altered in some way?

    a. CPT
    b. ICD-9-CM
    c. ICD-10-CM
    d. All of the choices

50. The _____ form is used by non-institutional providers and suppliers to bill Medicare, Part B covered services.

    a. HCPA-1000
    b. CPT
    c. CMS-1500
    d. UB92

II: Medical Terminology (MT)
A. Foundations of Word Structure
B. Abbreviations

Review Questions

1. The suffix *-emia* means _____.

    a. blood
    b. erudite
    c. hematemesis
    d. condition of the urine

2. The medical term for expanding or opening wider is _____.

    a. dysuria
    b. defamation
    c. dilate
    d. atelectasis

3. The abbreviation for urinalysis is _____.

    a. UA
    b. UN
    c. hystero
    d. urino

4. The medical term for groups of cells with the same function is _____.

    a. hormone
    b. artery
    c. system
    d. tissue

5. The medical term for the basic unit of body structure is _____.

    a. vein
    b. tissue
    c. cell
    d. organ

6. The abbreviation for below or low is _____.

    a. HUC
    b. hyper
    c. hypo
    d. post or p

7. The medical term for the time when menstruation begins is _____.

    a. menopause
    b. puberty
    c. menarche
    d. period

8. The medical term for the time when menstruation stops is _____.

    a. reflex
    b. growth
    c. menopause
    d. menarche

9. The abbreviation for gastrointestinal is _____.

    a. Gtt or G.T.T.
    b. Gyn. or G.Y.N.
    c. GI or G.I.
    d. abd.

10. The medical term for an involuntary movement is _____.

    a. growth
    b. reflex
    c. puberty
    d. stretching

11. The medical term for paralysis from the waist down is _____.

    a. coma
    b. quadriplegia
    c. disaster
    d. paraplegia

12. The medical term for paralysis from the neck down is _____.

    a. paraplegia
    b. quadriplegia
    c. hemiplegia
    d. stroke

13. The medical abbreviation for by mouth is _____.

    a. po
    b. PMC or P.M.C.
    c. pc
    d. per

14. The abbreviation for dressing is _____.

    a. dsg
    b. ds
    c. DSM
    d. DSS

15. The medical term for paralysis on one side of the body is _____.

    a. paraplegia
    b. coma
    c. hemiplegia
    d. quadriplegia

16. The medical term for circular movement around a central point is _____.

    a. extension
    b. rotation
    c. abduction
    d. dorsiflexion

17. The medical term for turning the palm forward, as applied to the hand is _____.

    a. extension
    b. flexion
    c. supination
    d. adduction

18. The medical term for a decrease in size or a wasting is _____.

    a. pronation
    b. atrophy
    c. plantar flexion
    d. abduction

19. The medical term for straightening of a body part is _____.

    a. extension
    b. flexion
    c. dorsiflexion
    d. pronation

20. The abbreviation for postprandial blood sugar is _____.

    a. PP
    b. pre
    c. PPBS
    d. post or p

21. The medical term for moving a body part away from the body is _____.

    a. rotation
    b. abduction
    c. dorsiflexion
    d. pronation

22. The medical term for bending a body part is _____.

    a. dorsiflexion
    b. external rotation
    c. flexion
    d. range-of-motion

23. The medical term for turning the palm backward is _____.

    a. pronation
    b. adduction
    c. external rotation
    d. supination

24. The medical term for bending backward is _____.

    a. contracture
    b. dorsiflexion
    c. hyperextension
    d. extension

25. The medical term for the abnormal shortening of a muscle is _____.

    a. adduction
    b. extension
    c. contracture
    d. flexion

26. The medical term for moving a body part toward the midline of the body is _____.

    a. flexion
    b. abduction
    c. adduction
    d. contracture

27. The abbreviation for laboratory is _____.

    a. lab
    b. L
    c. lbb
    d. lbt

28. The abbreviation for discontinue is _____.

    a. DD
    b. D. & C. or D&C
    c. DX
    d. d/c

29. The abbreviation for bedtime or hour of sleep is _____.

    a. ht
    b. b.m. or B.M.
    c. hs
    d. BSC or bsc

30. The abbreviation for above or high is _____.

    a. hyper
    b. approx
    c. hypo
    d. HS or hs

31. The abbreviation for hour is _____.

    a. ht
    b. HS or hs
    c. ord
    d. hr or h

32. The abbreviation for electroencephalogram is _____.

    a. EEG
    b. EKG
    c. ECG
    d. E

33. The abbreviation for Papanicolaou smear is _____.

    a. pap smear
    b. PS
    c. PPSM
    d. P smear

34. The abbreviation for cancer is _____.

    a. cc or c.c.
    b. CCU or C.C.U.
    c. CA
    d. C/O or c/o

35. The medical term for loss of appetite is _____.

    a. dehydration
    b. edema
    c. anorexia
    d. nutrient

36. The medical term for tube feeding is _____.

    a. IV
    b. gavage
    c. IVN
    d. esophageal introduction

37. The medical term for sugar in the urine is _____.

    a. glucosuria
    b. ketone body
    c. acetone
    d. catheter

38. The common term for a decubitus ulcer; a pressure sore is _____.

    a. blister
    b. pimple
    c. fever blister
    d. bedsore

39. The abbreviation for temperature, pulse, and respiration is _____.

    a. temp
    b. TPR
    c. trfc
    d. vtls

40. The word element *phlebo* means _____.

    a. vein
    b. breathing
    c. air, lungs
    d. alongside of

41. The word element *pneumo* means _____.

    a. disease
    b. air, lungs
    c. eye
    d. fear, dread

42. The word element *adeno* means _____.

    a. pain
    b. both
    c. gland
    d. anus

43. The word elements *algia, algesia* refer to _____.

    a. artery
    b. pain
    c. against
    d. air

44. The word element *cardio* means _____.

    a. gall
    b. colon
    c. heart
    d. cut

45. The word element *cranio* means _____.

    a. skull
    b. blood
    c. common bile duct
    d. cartilage

46. The word element *ectomy* means _____.

    a. air
    b. outer, on the outside
    c. surgical removal
    d. no correct answer

47. The word element *emesis* means _____.

    a. vomiting
    b. kill
    c. weakness
    d. no correct answer

48. The word element *cise* means _____.

    a. colon
    b. cut
    c. tumor, swelling, hernia, sac
    d. no correct answer

49. The word element *centesis* means _____.

    a. slow
    b. common bile duct
    c. cell
    d. puncture

50. The word element *renal* means _____.

    a. kidney
    b. flow
    c. nose
    d. no correct answer

51. The word element *post* means _____.

    a. pus
    b. before
    c. after
    d. too few

52. The word element *osis* means _____.

    a. tumor
    b. eye
    c. condition of
    d. ear

53. The word element *rhino* means _____.

    a. ear
    b. nose
    c. throat
    d. eye

54. The word element *stomato* means _____.

    a. mouth or the ostium uteri
    b. upper intestine
    c. psychogenic symptoms
    d. gallstones

55. The word element *super* means _____.

    a. great
    b. above
    c. study of
    d. no correct answer

56. The abbreviation for toxic shock syndrome is _____.

    a. TSS
    b. tox
    c. tsx
    d. txs

57. Erythema refers to _____.

    a. blue skin
    b. red skin
    c. gray skin
    d. yellow skin

58. The opposite of deep is _____.

    a. superficial
    b. low
    c. proximal
    d. no correct answer

59. High blood pressure is referred to as _____.

    a. palpitation
    b. hypertension
    c. bradycardia
    d. tachycardia

60. Neoplasm refers to _____.

    a. above
    b. new growth
    c. cut into
    d. liver

61. The abbreviation *carb* means _____.

    a. carbolic
    b. computer aided sleep system
    c. carbohydrate
    d. no correct answer

62. The abbreviation for chief complaint is _____.

    a. CC
    b. ccom
    c. chf
    d. CCFD

63. The abbreviation for grain is _____.

    a. gr
    b. g
    c. gn
    d. grn

III. Pharmacology (PH)
Administration of Medication

Review Questions

1. What license must a physician have to dispense, prescribe, or administer controlled substances?

    a. Lawyers
    b. Narcotics
    c. Business
    d. Occupational

2. Physicians with a narcotics license are required to register on June 30 of each year with _____.

    a. Food and Drug Administration
    b. Drug Enforcement Agency
    c. American Red Cross
    d. American Medical Association

3. A drug that causes urination is called a(n) _____.

    a. diuretic
    b. emetic
    c. cirrhotic
    d. esculent

4. A drug used to relieve a cough is called a(n) _____.

    a. antitussive
    b. bronchodilator
    c. antiseptic
    d. antitoxin

5. A drug that neutralizes acidity is called a(n) _____.

    a. antidiarrhetic
    b. antinauseant
    c. antacid
    d. placebo

6. A drug that controls appetite is called a(n) _____.

   a. appetite suppressor
   b. appetite stimulant
   c. antispasmodic
   d. appetite placebo

7. A drug used to prevent blood from clotting is called a(n) _____.

   a. anticholinergic
   b. anticoagulant
   c. antidote
   d. placebo

8. A drug used to control temperature is called an _____.

   a. antipyretic
   b. antidote
   c. anticoagulant
   d. analgesic

9. A drug that reduces anxiety is called a(n) _____.

   a. diuretic
   b. tranquilizer
   c. vaccine
   d. ointment

10. A drug that causes dilation of blood vessels is called a _____.

    a. vasodilator
    b. vasoconstrictor
    c. sedative
    d. laxative

11. A drug that decreases congestion is called a _____.

    a. suppressant
    b. decongestant
    c. diuretic
    d. sedative

12. A drug that causes the pupil of the eye to dilate is called a _____.

    a. myotic
    b. mydriatic
    c. placebo
    d. vaccine

13. A date on a bottle of medication that provides a "use until" date is the _____.

    a. manufacture's date
    b. outdate or expiration date
    c. "sell by" date
    d. ingredient half-life date

14. A drug that increases urinary output is called a(n) _____.

    a. miotic
    b. diuretic
    c. cytotoxin
    d. expectorant

15. A liquid preparation which mixes fine droplets of an oil in water, such as castor oil, is called a(n) _____.

    a. solution
    b. emulsion
    c. elixir
    d. tinctures

16. Nitroglycerine is used for _____.

    a. narcotic overdose
    b. inflammatory conditions
    c. treatment of angina pectoris
    d. anti-anxiety muscle relaxant treatment

17. Hydrocortisone is a drug used to suppress _____.

    a. inflammation
    b. appetite
    c. swelling
    d. excretion of urine

18. Schedule I drugs include _____.

    a. miscellaneous mixtures containing limited amounts of narcotic drugs
    b. substances that have no accepted medical use and a high potential for abuse
    c. minor tranquilizers and hypnotics that have a lesser potential for abuse
    d. no correct answer

19. Schedule IV drugs include _____.

    a. includes various narcotics such as opium
    b. substances that have no accepted medical use and a high potential for abuse
    c. minor tranquilizers and hypnotics that have a lesser potential for abuse
    d. no correct answer

20. A small adhesive patch or disc used for administration of drugs is called a(n) _____.

    a. transdermal system
    b. reservoir system
    c. ointment system
    d. epidermis system

21. The buccal method of administering a drug is done by _____.

    a. placing the medication between the gum and cheek
    b. inhalation
    c. intramuscular injection
    d. intravenous solution

22. Oxygen is ordered as percentage of oxygen concentration and its rate of delivery is written as _____.

    a. liters per minute
    b. volume per minute
    c. degrees per minute
    d. percentage per minute

23. A drug that produces sleep is called a(n) _____.

    a. placebo
    b. hypnotic
    c. antispasmodic
    d. diaphoretic

24. An inactive substance substituted in place of the actual drug to satisfy the patient is called a(n) _____.

    a. sedative
    b. stimulant
    c. placebo
    d. antiseptic

25. The abbreviation for elixir is _____.

    a. elix
    b. exr
    c. elx
    d. EX

26. The abbreviation for emulsion is _____.

    a. emul
    b. eml
    c. els
    d. EML

27. The abbreviation for fluid is _____.

    a. fl or fld
    b. wet
    c. flud
    d. fuid

28. The abbreviation for ointment is _____.

    a. ont
    b. oint, ung
    c. ONT
    d. cream

29. The abbreviation for solution is _____.

    a. sol
    b. slt
    c. stn
    d. SSN

30. The abbreviation for suppository is _____.

    a. supp
    b. supt
    c. SSUP
    d. SPT

31. The abbreviation for syrup is _____.

    a. sup
    b. syr
    c. spp
    d. syp

32. The abbreviation for tablet is _____.

    a. tbb
    b. tsp
    c. tbl
    d. tab

33. The abbreviation for tincture is _____.

    a. tcc
    b. tinc
    c. tct
    d. tcr

34. The abbreviation for intramuscular is _____.

    a. IM
    b. ims
    c. IMSC
    d. imul

35. The abbreviation for injection is _____.

    a. in
    b. inj
    c. ing
    d. ij

36. The abbreviation for right ear is _____.

    a. AD
    b. RE
    c. re
    d. rter

37. The abbreviation for both ears is _____.

    a. AU
    b. BE
    c. bthe
    d. BERS

38. The abbreviation for drops is _____.

    a. gtt
    b. dtt
    c. gts
    d. dts

39. The abbreviation for two times a day is _____.

    a. tid
    b. bid
    c. qid
    d. qh

40. When mixing reagents always read the label _____.

    a. with the doctor
    b. with a nurse
    c. with magnifying glasses
    d. twice

41. The _____ pages of the Physician's Desk Reference is where a medical assistant would be able to locate a medication by brand or generic name.

    a. white
    b. blue
    c. pink
    d. gray

42. Medications can be located in the Physician's Drug reference under all of the following categories EXCEPT _____.

    a. manufacturer
    b. generic name
    c. classification
    d. composition

43. The physician has ordered 500 mg. of a medication the amount on hand is 250mg per tablet. How many tablets will be given?

    a. 0.5 tab
    b. 1 tab
    c. 2 tab
    d. 2.5 tab

44. The physician has ordered 0.2 Gm of a medication. The amount on hand is 400 mg tabs. How many tablets will be given to the patient?

    a. 0.5 tab
    b. 1 tab
    c. 2 tab
    d. 2.5 tab

45. The physician has ordered 50 mg of Demerol be given to a patient. The amount of hand is 100mg/ml. How many cc's of Demerol will be injected?

    a. 0.5 cc
    b. 1 cc
    c. 1.5 cc
    d. 0.25 cc

IV. Anatomy & Physiology (AN)

Review Questions

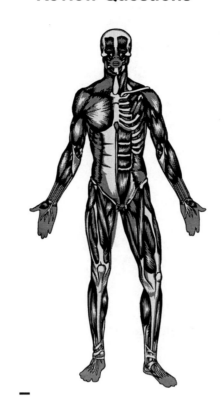

1. The sebaceous glands, skin, hair, and nails make up the _____ system.

    a. nervous
    b. cardiovascular
    c. sensory
    d. integumentary

2. The heart, lymphatic organs, and blood vessels are in the _____ system.

    a. respiratory
    b. cardiovascular
    c. digestive
    d. urinary

3. The liver, stomach, mouth, and pancreas are in the _____ system.

    a. reproductive
    b. sensory
    c. digestive
    d. muscular

4. The bladder, urethra, kidneys, and ureters are in the _____ system.

   a. urinary
   b. reproductive
   c. respiratory
   d. muscular

5. In the human body, the senses include all of the following EXCEPT _____.

   a. ears
   b. eyes
   c. teeth
   d. nose

6. The brain, nerves, and spinal cord are in the _____ system.

   a. skeletal
   b. nervous
   c. sensory
   d. endocrine

7. The trachea, nose, lungs, and pharynx are in the _____ system.

   a. skeletal
   b. respiratory
   c. nervous
   d. sensory

8. Tendons, joints, bones, and cartilages are in the _____ system.

   a. skeletal
   b. integumentary
   c. muscular
   d. endocrine

9. The upper middle area of the abdomen is called the _____.

   a. hypogastric region
   b. epigastric region
   c. umbilical region
   d. no correct answer

10. The lower middle area of the abdomen is called the _____.

    a. hypogastric region
    b. epigastric region
    c. umbilical region
    d. no correct answer

11. The central middle area of the abdomen is called the _____.

    a. hypogastric region
    b. epigastric region
    c. umbilical region
    d. No correct answer

12. The humerus is located in the _____.

    a. leg
    b. arm
    c. back
    d. neck

13. The pubis is located in the _____.

    a. pelvis
    b. chest
    c. neck
    d. foot

14. The femur is located in the _____.

    a. leg
    b. arm
    c. foot
    d. neck

15. The patella is located in the _____.

    a. knee
    b. elbow
    c. neck
    d. head

16. The ulna is located in the _____.

    a. back
    b. foot
    c. leg
    d. arm

17. The tibia is located in the _____.

    a. foot
    b. arm
    c. back
    d. leg

18. The fibula is located in the _____.

    a. leg
    b. arm
    c. foot
    d. hand

19. The radius is located in the _____.

    a. arm
    b. leg
    c. foot
    d. hand

20. The maxilla is located in the _____.

    a. head
    b. foot
    c. chest
    d. arm

21. The metatarsals are located in the _____.

    a. foot
    b. hand
    c. leg
    d. arm

22. The metacarpals are located in the _____.

    a. foot
    b. hand
    c. back
    d. chest

23. The name for the collar bone is _____.

    a. carpals
    b. clavicle
    c. fossa
    d. femur

24. The smaller of the lower leg bones is called _____.

    a. fibula
    b. tibia
    c. patella
    d. femur

25. The zygomatic bone is located in the _____.

    a. head
    b. chest
    c. leg
    d. knee

26. The mandible bone is located in the _____.

    a. chest
    b. head
    c. foot
    d. leg

27. The sphenoid bone is located in the _____.

    a. foot
    b. chest
    c. leg
    d. head

28. The vertebrae are located in the _____.

    a. head
    b. back
    c. leg
    d. arm

29. Bones are _____.

    a. meant to be pliable and bend easily
    b. built to provide support & structure
    c. filled with carbon dioxide
    d. solid, sturdy calcium structures

30. The study of bones is called _____.

    a. osteology
    b. morphology
    c. neurology
    d. No corrcct answer

31. The majority of the bones in the arms and legs are _____ bones.

    a. short
    b. long
    c. flat
    d. irregular

32. Bones of the wrist and ankle are called _____ bones.

    a. long
    b. short
    c. flat
    d. sesamoid

33. The muscle that flexes and supinates the forearm is called _____.

    a. deltoid
    b. biceps brachii
    c. rectus femoris
    d. vastus lateralis

34. The major artery to the head is called the _____.

    a. brachial
    b. carotid
    c. ulnar
    d. renal

35. One of the arteries that supplies the hand and forearm is called the _____.

    a. intercostal
    b. ulnar
    c. brachial
    d. renal

36. The major artery that supplies the abdomen is called the _____ artery.

    a. celiac
    b. carotid
    c. brachial
    d. iliac

37. The major artery that supplies the thorax is called the _____ artery.

    a. renal
    b. intercostal
    c. radial
    d. aorta

38. The major artery that supplies the kidney is called the _____ artery.

    a. celiac
    b. renal
    c. ulnar
    d. brachial

39. The major artery that supplies the bladder, rectum, and some reproductive organs is called the _____.

    a. iliac
    b. celiac
    c. carotid
    d. ulnar

40. The major artery that supplies the upper arm is called the _____.

    a. brachial
    b. carotid
    c. ulnar
    d. iliac

41. The major artery that supplies the knee is called the _____.

    a. popliteal
    b. dorsalis pedis
    c. ulnar
    d. carotid

42. The major artery that supplies the foot is called the _____.

    a. dorsalis pedis
    b. popliteal
    c. iliac
    d. renal

43. The major vein that drains the upper arm is called the _____.

    a. jugular
    b. brachial
    c. cephalic
    d. femoral

44. The major vein that drains blood from the head and brain is called the _____.

    a. jugular
    b. vertebral
    c. cephalic
    d. ulnar

45. The major vein that drains the liver is called the _____.

    a. hepatic
    b. axillary
    c. ulnar
    d. femoral

46. The major vein that drains the kidneys is called the _____.

    a. hepatic
    b. renal
    c. cephalic
    d. femoral

47. The major vein that drains the pelvis is called the _____.

    a. common iliac
    b. hepatic
    c. renal
    d. ulnar

48. The point at which air enters the respiratory tract is called the _____.

    a. larynx
    b. lung
    c. nasal cavity
    d. bronchus

49. The wind pipe which conducts air between the larynx and lungs is called the _____.

    a. larynx
    b. pharynx
    c. trachea
    d. lungs

50. The divisions of the trachea which enter the lungs are called the _____.

    a. pharynx
    b. trachea
    c. bronchi
    d. larynx

51. Located between the pharynx and trachea, and containing the vocal cords is the _____.

    a. larynx
    b. pharynx
    c. nasal cavity
    d. trachea

52. A condition of the nasal septum turning away from midline is called a _____.

    a. sinusitis
    b. deviated septum
    c. dislocated sinus
    d. nasal polyp

53. The medical name for nose bleed is called _____.

    a. epistaxis
    b. sinusitis
    c. pleurisy
    d. coryza

54. Inflammation of the sinus cavity is called _____.

    a. sinusitis
    b. epistaxis
    c. asthma
    d. emphysema

55. Inflammation of the pleura is called _____.

    a. pneumonia
    b. pleurisy
    c. atelectasis
    d. pleural effusion

56. Escape of fluid into the thoracic cavity is called _____.

    a. pulmonary edema
    b. pleural effusion
    c. emphysema
    d. pneumonia

57. Inflammation of the nasal mucosa results in _____.

    a. nasal polyps
    b. sinusitis
    c. rhinitis
    d. pleurisy

58. An accumulation of air in the pleural cavity after the lungs collapse is known as _____.

    a. pneumonia
    b. pneumothorax
    c. asthma
    d. pleural effusion

59. Whooping cough is another name for _____.

    a. croup
    b. pertussis
    c. pleurisy
    d. pneumonia

60. Inflammation of the mucus lining of the vagina is called _____.

    a. phlegmon
    b. vaginitis
    c. pyorrhea
    d. thrush

61. Inflammation of the gums is called _____.

    a. stomatitis
    b. gingivitis
    c. dental inflammation
    d. thrush

62. Lesions of the mucous membrane of the stomach are called _____ ulcers.

    a. gastric
    b. intestinal
    c. duodenal
    d. follicular

63. A serious chronic disease of the liver is called _____.

    a. hiatal hernia
    b. cirrhosis
    c. cholecystitis
    d. pancreatitis

64. Chronic inflammation of the colon is called _____.

    a. colitis
    b. colonitis
    c. pancreatitis
    d. no correct answer

65. Inflammation of the gallbladder is called _____.

    a. cystitis
    b. colitis
    c. diverticulitis
    d. cholecystitis

66. Inflammation of the pancreas is called _____.

    a. pancreatitis
    b. colitis
    c. diverticulitis
    d. cholecystitis

67. Inflammation of the appendix is called _____.

   a. pancreatitis
   b. appendicitis
   c. cholecystitis
   d. diverticulitis

68. Dilated veins that occur in the rectum are known as _____.

   a. hemorrhoids
   b. hepatitis
   c. hernias
   d. no correct answer

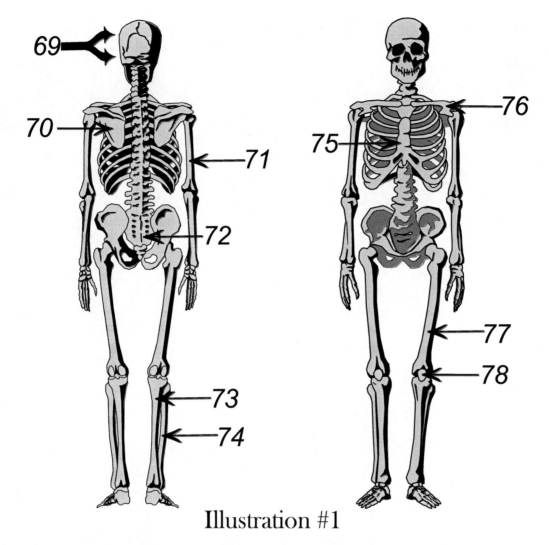

Illustration #1

69. Referring to Illustration #1, identify the number 69.

   a. Nasal
   b. Zygomatic
   c. Temporal
   d. Radius

70. Referring to Illustration #1, identify the number 70.

   a. Clavicle
   b. Sternum
   c. Scapula
   d. Ilium

71. Referring to Illustration #1, identify the number 71.

   a. Radius
   b. Clavicle
   c. Humerus
   d. Ulna

72. Referring to Illustration # 1, identify the number 72.

    a. Femur
    b. Sacrum
    c. Ilium
    d. Coccyx

73. Referring to Illustration # 1, identify the number 73.

    a. Tibia
    b. Femur
    c. Fibula
    d. Patella

74. Referring to Illustration # 1, identify the number 74.

    a. Talus
    b. Femur
    c. Tibia
    d. Fibula

75. Referring to Illustration # 1, identify the number 75.

    a. Scapula
    b. Sternum
    c. Clavicle
    d. Maxilla

76. Referring to Illustration # 1, identify the number 76.

    a. Clavicle
    b. Humerus
    c. Sternum
    d. Sacrum

77. Referring to Illustration # 1, identify the number 77.

    a. Femur
    b. Sacrum
    c. Patella
    d. Fibula

78. Referring to Illustration # 1, identify the number 78.

    a. Talus
    b. Phalanges
    c. Patella
    d. Metatarsals

79. When the internal environment of the body is functioning properly, a condition of _____ exists.

    a. homeostasis
    b. dysfunction
    c. hemorrhage
    d. euphoria

80. The science of the function of cells, tissues, and organs of the body is called _____.

    a. physiology
    b. anatomy
    c. histology
    d. gross anatomy

81. The lateral movement of the limbs away from the median plane of the body, is called _____.

    a. extension
    b. internal rotation
    c. abduction
    d. supination

82. An extrauterine pregnancy in which the fertilized ovum begins to develop outside the uterus is called _____.

    a. eclampsia
    b. toxemia
    c. ectopic
    d. PID

83. The second portion of the small intestine is called the _____.

    a. decalvant
    b. sigmoid
    c. duodenum
    d. jejunum

84. One of the vital functions of long bones is the formation of _____.

    a. white blood cells
    b. red blood cells
    c. calcium
    d. cellulite

85. A unilateral paralysis that follows damage to the brain is called _____.

    a. hemiplegia
    b. quadriplegia
    c. paraplegia
    d. sciatica

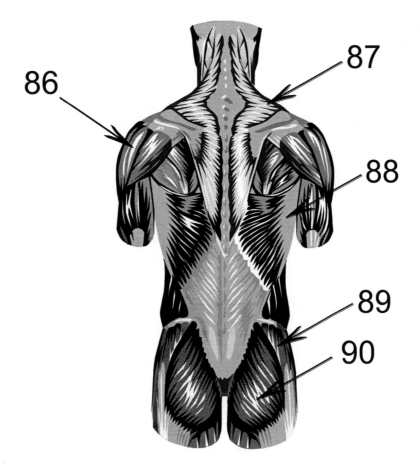

Illustration #2

86. Referring to Illustration #2, identify number 86.

   a. Trapezius
   b. Deltoid
   c. Triceps brachii
   d. Pectoralis major

87. Referring to Illustration #2, identify number 87.

   a. Zygomatic
   b. Brachialis
   c. Trapezius
   d. Sternocleidomastoid

88. Referring to Illustration #2, identify number 88.

   a. Brachioradialis
   b. External oblique
   c. Teres major
   d. Latissimus dorsi

89. Referring to Illustration #2, identify number 89.

    a. Semitendinosus
    b. Piriformis
    c. Adductor magnus
    d. Gluteus medius

90. Referring to Illustration #2, identify number 90.

    a. Gluteus maximus
    b. Gracilis
    c. Transversus abdominis
    d. Adductor magnus

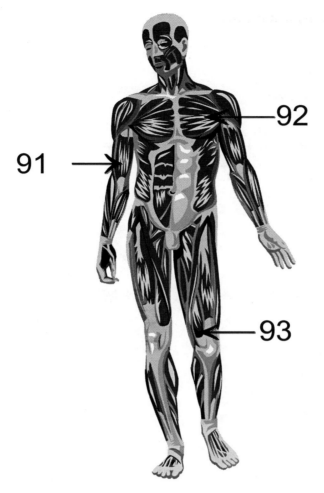

Illustration #3

91. Referring to Illustration #3, identify number 91.

   a. Deltoid
   b. Biceps brachii
   c. Trapezius
   d. Brachioradialis

92. Referring to Illustration #3, identify number. 92.

   a. Deltoid
   b. Biceps brachii
   c. Trapezius
   d. Pectoralis major

93. Referring to Illustration #3, identify number 93.

   a. Quadriceps femoris
   b. Sartoris
   c. Tibialis anterior
   d. Peroneus longus

94. The use of ultrasound to produce a picture of the structure of the heart is called _____.

    a. cardiac catheterization
    b. a cardiac stress test
    c. echocardiography
    d. electrocardiography

95. Digestion begins in the mouth, where food is chewed and mixed with a substance called _____.

    a. amino acid
    b. saliva
    c. fatty acid
    d. no correct answer

96. The lining of the duodenum is composed of thousands of tiny finger-like projections called _____.

    a. ulcers
    b. villi
    c. hemorrhoids
    d. hernias

97. Infected pressure sores on the skin are called _____.

    a. decubitus ulcers
    b. carbuncles
    c. furuncles
    d. decubitus blisters

98. Varicose veins of the anal canal or outside the external sphincter are called _____.

    a. hemorrhoids
    b. villi
    c. peritonitis
    d. diarrhea

99. Carcinogenic means _____ causing.

    a. diarrhea
    b. disease
    c. cough
    d. cancer

100. A weakness in the walls of muscle that allows underlying tissue to push through it is called _____.

    a. an ulcer
    b. a hernia
    c. a hemorrhoid
    d. diarrhea

101. A gallbladder disorder involving stones in the gallbladder is _____.

    a. cholecystitis
    b. intestinal obstruction
    c. hepatitis
    d. cholelithiasis

102. Inflammation of the retina is _____.

    a. retinitis
    b. peritonitis
    c. colitis
    d. hernia

103. Foods that are mild in flavor and easy to digest (non-spicy) comprise a _____.

    a. clear liquid diet
    b. low calorie diet
    c. diabetic diet
    d. bland diet

104. A tube inserted into one of the patient's nostrils and down the back of the throat, through the esophagus until the end reaches the patient's stomach is a(n) _____.

    a. test tube
    b. nasogastric tube
    c. irrigation tube
    d. no correct answer

105. Washing out of the stomach through a nasogastric tube is called _____.

    a. gavage
    b. lavage
    c. both a and b
    d. no correct answer

106. The healthy adult excretes daily approximately _____ of urine.

    a. 1000 to 1500 milliliters
    b. 5 to 100 milliliters
    c. 4000 to 6000 milliliters
    d. 100 to 500 milliliters

107. The inability to control the passage of urine in the bladder is called _____.

    a. specimen
    b. urine analysis
    c. urinary incontinence
    d. dripping

108. Painful voiding is called _____.

    a. urine burn
    b. dysuria
    c. hydronephrosis
    d. cystitis

109. If the septum of the heart has an abnormal opening it is referred to as _____.

    a. stenosis
    b. a septal defect
    c. phlebitis
    d. a heart murmur

110. Branches of the bundle branches, which transmit the impulses to the walls of the ventricles, causing the ventricles to contract are called _____.

    a. bundle of his
    b. purkinje fibers
    c. left bundle branches
    d. right bundle branches

111. A coronary occlusion causing a condition that produces chest pain which may radiate to the left arm, shoulder, jaw or neck due to lack of blood supply to the heart is called _____.

    a. angina pectoris
    b. arteriolosclerosis
    c. atherosclerosis
    d. hypertension

112. An obstruction of a coronary artery causing death of an area of the myocardium due to blockage of blood supply and oxygen supply is called _____.

    a. hypertension
    b. myocardial infarction
    c. arteriosclerosis
    d. primary hypertension

113. Deoxygenated blood enters the right atrium of the _____.

    a. vena cava
    b. lung
    c. heart
    d. pharynx

114. When the right atrium contracts it forces blood through the tricuspid valve into the _____ ventricle.

    a. left
    b. top
    c. right
    d. inner

115. The right ventricle pumps the used blood to the lungs by way of the _____ artery.

    a. superior
    b. vena cava
    c. pulmonary
    d. atria

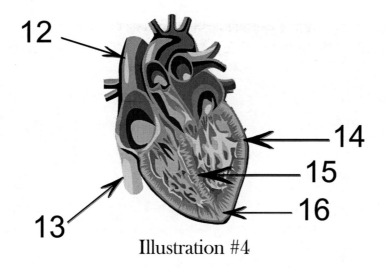
Illustration #4

Figure 1

116. Referring to Illustration #4, identify number 12.

    a. Pulmonary vein
    b. Superior vena cava
    c. Aorta
    d. Right atrium

117. Referring to Illustration #4, identify number 13.

    a. Inferior vena cava
    b. Superior vena cava
    c. Left pulmonary artery
    d. Aorta

118. Referring to Illustration #4, identify number 14.

    a. Purkinje fibers
    b. Interventricular septum
    c. Myocardium
    d. Apex

119. Referring to Illustration #4, identify number 15.

    a. Apex
    b. Tricuspid valve
    c. Interventricular septum
    d. Endocardium

120. Referring to Illustration #4, identify number 16.

    a. Apex
    b. Endocardium
    c. Aorta
    d. Interventricular septum

V. Medical Procedures
A. Infection Control, Exposure Control, and Safety

Review Questions

The information in this chapter regarding blood borne pathogens was obtained from 29CFR1910.1030. We recommend that if you have any questions concerning the material covered, contact your local, federal government bookstore for the December 6th, 1991 federal register volume 56, no. 235, pages 63861 – 64186, and later updates in the law.

1. Every medical facility is required by OSHA to have an exposure control plan.

    a. True
    b. False

2. The exposure control plan shall be made available to the Assistant Secretary and the Director OSHA upon request for examination and copying.

    a. True
    b. False

3. "HIV" means _____.

    a. hepatitis B virus
    b. hepatitis C virus
    c. human immunodeficiency virus
    d. human infectious virus

4. _____ mean any contaminated objects that can penetrate the skin including, but not limited to needles, scalpels, broken glass, broken capillary tubes, and exposed ends of dental wires.

    a. "Contaminated Devices"
    b. "Disposable Devices"
    c. "Contaminated Sharps"
    d. "Dangerous Incisor"

5. Reasonable anticipated skin, eye, mucous membrane, or parenteral contact with blood, or other potentially infectious materials that may result from the performance of an employee's duties is called _____.

    a. occupational exposure
    b. daily risk
    c. occupational risk
    d. professional threat

6. Any individual, living or dead, whose blood, or other potentially infectious materials may be a source of occupational exposure to the employee is called a(n) _____.

    a. hazardous individual
    b. source individual
    c. infected specimen
    d. quarantined source

7. To use a physical chemical procedure to destroy all microbial life including highly resistant bacterial endospores is to _____.

    a. eradicate
    b. detoxify
    c. sterilize
    d. acid wash

8. _____ is the single most important source of HIV and HBV in the workplace.

    a. Semen
    b. Saliva in dental procedures
    c. Pleural fluid
    d. Blood

9. The risk of infection with HIV following one needle-stick exposure to blood from a patient known to be infected with HIV is approximately _____.

    a. 0.01%
    b. 0.50%
    c. 1.00%
    d. 5.00%

10. General infection-control procedures are designed to prevent transmission of a wide range of _____ and to provide a wide margin of safety in the varied situations encountered in the health-care environment.

    a. diseases
    b. conditions
    c. microbiological agents
    d. sickness

11. "Contact with blood, or other body fluids to which universal precautions apply through percutaneous inoculation, or contact with an open wound, non-intact skin, or mucous membrane during the performance of normal duties" this definition (found in the Federal Register) applies to _____.

    a. human exposure
    b. exposed worker
    c. worker stress
    d. stressed worker

12. All workers whose jobs involve participation in tasks, or activities with exposure to blood, or other body fluids to which universal precautions apply, should be vaccinated with _____ vaccine.

    a. human immunodeficiency
    b. hepatitis C
    c. small pox
    d. hepatitis B

13. _____ testing should be made available by the employer to all workers who maybe concerned they have been infected with HIV through an occupational exposure.

    a. Serologic
    b. Blood
    c. Immediate
    d. Bacterial

14. Studies suggest that the potential for salivary transmission of HIV is _____.

    a. frequent
    b. 25%
    c. remote
    d. as frequent as blood transmission

15. After they are used, disposable syringes and needles, scalpel blades, and other sharp items should be placed in _____ containers for disposal.

    a. biodegradable
    b. puncture-resistant
    c. OSHA
    d. sanitized

16. Broken glassware which may be contaminated shall not be picked up directly with the hands, but by mechanical means, such as _____.

    a. by a lab technician
    b. an evacuated tube
    c. a brush and dust pan
    d. gloved hands

17. Contaminated laundry shall be _____ where it was soiled.

    a. destroyed at the location
    b. transported away from the location
    c. disinfected or discarded at the location
    d. bagged or containerized at the location

18. All spills of blood-contaminated fluids should be promptly cleaned up using _____ approved germicide, or a 1:10 solution of household bleach.

    a. an OSHA
    b. an EPA
    c. a hospital or clinic
    d. a consumer

19. In cases of blood contamination shoe coverings and gloves should be disposed of in _____ biohazard plastic bags.

    a. black
    b. clearly marked
    c. orange-red
    d. transparent

20. It is recommended that protective masks and eye wear, or face shields, be worn by laboratory technicians, or housekeeping personnel _____.

    a. when cleaning up blood or body fluids
    b. at all times in the laboratory
    c. when routinely cleaning equipment
    d. when scrubbing laboratory floors

21. Blood from all individuals should be considered _____.

    a. decontaminated
    b. infective or infectious
    c. biodegradable
    d. chemically hazardous

22. When taking vital signs, a medical assistant must wear gloves, gowns, and eye wear.

    a. True
    b. False

23. A specific eye, mouth, other mucous membrane, non-intact skin, or parenteral contact with blood, or other potentially infectious materials that results from the performance of an employees duties is called _____.

    a. unfortunate incident
    b. hazardous exposure
    c. occupational hazard
    d. exposure incident

24. The term "Universal Precautions" is an _____.

    a. organization to promote infection control
    b. overall approach to infection control
    c. organizational approach to following EPA guidelines
    d. abbreviation for World Health Organization standards

25. Vaccinations against HBV infection provide 90% protection against hepatitis B for _____ or more years following vaccination.

    a. seven
    b. ten
    c. four
    d. twelve

26. The first line of defense in preventing disease is _____.

    a. wearing a mask
    b. the medical hand wash
    c. wearing gloves
    d. wearing a gown

27. Biohazard labels must be colored _____.

    a. blue
    b. orange-red
    c. green
    d. grey-black

28. What federal agency requires the use of Sharps Containers?

    a. Occupational Safety and Health Administration
    b. Drug Enforcement Agency
    c. Department of Defense
    d. Law Enforcement Agency

29. Viruses can reproduce only in _____.

    a. dead cells
    b. living cells
    c. both dead and living cells
    d. no correct answer

30. The process of killing all microorganisms in a certain area is called _____.

    a. disinfection
    b. washing
    c. sterilization
    d. dusting

31. The autoclave sterilizes or completely destroys microorganism by combining _____.

    a. bleach and water under pressure
    b. acid with steam
    c. heat with steam under pressure
    d. hot water and soap

32. What kind of environment do microorganisms grow best in?

    a. Cool and light
    b. Warm and light
    c. Cool and dark
    d. Dark and warm

33. A disease state that results from the invasion and growth of microorganisms in the body is _____.

    a. a syndrome
    b. an infection
    c. a laceration
    d. an asepsis

34. Practices to achieve asepsis are known as _____.

    a. medical asepsis
    b. contamination
    c. clean technique
    d. both a and c

35. The process by which an object or area becomes unclean is _____.

    a. contamination
    b. disinfection
    c. sterilization
    d. heat

36. You should wash your hands for approximately _____.

    a. 15 to 20 seconds
    b. 1 to 2 minutes
    c. 10 minutes
    d. 5 minutes

37. When you wash your hands you should stand _____.

    a. up against the sink
    b. five inches from the sink
    c. so your clothes do not touch the sink
    d. no correct answer

38. The faucet is turned off with _____.

    a. your arm
    b. a paper towel
    c. your hand
    d. no correct answer

39. A health care worker who unconsciously transports harmful bacteria but is not ill is called a(n) _____.

    a. pre-infected
    b. carrier
    c. infectious
    d. immune

40. Groups or clusters of bacteria taken for laboratory study are called _____.

    a. families
    b. fungi
    c. cultures
    d. viruses (viri)

41. The patient with an infection may have _____.

    a. loss of appetite and fatigue
    b. fever, nausea, rash and vomiting
    c. pain, redness or swelling
    d. all answers are correct

42. Diseases that can be communicated from one person to another are called _____.

    a. catching
    b. contagious
    c. germicides
    d. decontaminated

43. When using a fire extinguisher the hose should be directed to the _____.

    a. middle of the fire
    b. top of the fire
    c. around the fire
    d. base of the fire

44. Aerobic bacteria prefer which of these environmental conditions to grow well?

    a. Increased nitrogen concentration
    b. An extremely dry environment
    c. Oxygen
    d. Temperature <100° Fahrenheit

V. Medical Procedures
B. Patient Examination and Clinical Skills

Review Questions

1. How quickly will an electronic thermometer measure body temperature?

    a. 7 to 8 minutes
    b. 3 minutes
    c. 2 to 60 seconds
    d. 5 minutes

2. Which of the following locations is usually used for taking a pulse?

    a. Apical pulse
    b. Radial pulse
    c. Brachial pulse
    d. Apical-radial pulse

3. What is considered a normal adult pulse rate?

    a. 70-170
    b. 90-130
    c. 70-80
    d. 60-100

4. The radial pulse is located in the _____.

    a. chest
    b. neck
    c. wrist
    d. head

5. The least reliable measurement of body temperature is _____.

    a. rectal
    b. oral
    c. axillary
    d. All are equally reliable

6. The most accurate and reliable measurement of body temperature is _____.

   a. rectal
   b. oral
   c. axillary
   d. nasal

7. What is considered a normal adult respiration per minute?

   a. 14 to 20
   b. 5 to 10
   c. 25 to 30
   d. No correct answer

8. A respiratory rate greater than 24 per minute is called _____.

   a. apnea
   b. hypoventilation
   c. tachypnea
   d. bradypnea

9. Persistent increased systolic and diastolic pressures are indicative of _____.

   a. hypotension
   b. hypertension
   c. normal
   d. no correct answer

10. The blood pressure should not be taken on an arm if _____.

    a. the patient has had breast surgery on that side
    b. on an arm with an IV infusion
    c. on an arm with a cast
    d. all answers are correct

11. To measure a blood pressure, the medical assistant will need _____.

    a. a stethoscope and sphygmomanometer
    b. a thermometer
    c. a mercury manometer
    d. to clean the area first

12. Which is recorded as the systolic blood pressure?

    a. The point where the first sound is heard
    b. The point where the last sound is heard
    c. Anything under 100 on the sphygmomanometer
    d. Anything over 100 on the sphygmomanometer

13. When measuring blood pressure, which of the following is correct?

    a. The cuff should be applied to the bare upper arm
    b. Room should be quiet so that blood pressure can be heard
    c. Sphygmomanometer needs to clearly visible
    d. All answers are correct

14. With vital signs, any abnormal measurement must be immediately reported to the _____.

    a. patient
    b. physician
    c. receptionist
    d. chart

15. A medical assistant would measure the patient's temperature, pulse and respiration when the physician asks him or her to _____.

    a. take blood pressure
    b. take three
    c. take vital signs
    d. all answers are correct

16. Which of the following is used to take an infant's rectal temperature?

    a. Oral thermometer
    b. Axillary thermometer
    c. Security thermometer
    d. No correct answer

17. Never clean a glass thermometer with _____.

    a. disinfectant
    b. cold water
    c. alcohol
    d. hot water

18. When the patient is breathing with only the upper part of the lungs this is referred to as _____.

    a. shallow respiration
    b. Cheyne-Stokes respiration
    c. stertorous respiration
    d. abdominal respiration

19. When the patient makes abnormal noises like snoring sounds when s/he is breathing, it is called _____.

    a. Cheyne-Stokes respiration
    b. irregular respiration
    c. abdominal respiration
    d. stertorous respiration

20. When the heart is contracting, the pressure is highest. This pressure is called the _____.

    a. systolic pressure
    b. diastolic pressure
    c. air pressure
    d. high pressure

21. When listening to the brachial pulse you will use a(n) _____.

    a. sphygmomanometer
    b. earphone
    c. stethoscope
    d. radio

22. The main type of sphygmomanometers used in a clinical setting is the _____.

    a. mercury type
    b. alcohol type
    c. aneroid type
    d. no correct answer is correct

23. When the pressure is lowest, this pressure is called _____.

    a. diastolic pressure
    b. air pressure
    c. systolic pressure
    d. water pressure

24. The process of inhaling and exhaling is called _____.

    a. temperature
    b. pulse
    c. respiration
    d. coughing

25. When the depth of breathing changes and the rate of the rise and fall of the chest is not steady, it is called _____.

    a. abdominal respiration
    b. stertorous respiration
    c. shallow respiration
    d. irregular respiration

26. When taking the pulse, you must be able to report accurately the _____.

    a. rhythm of pulse beats
    b. rate (number of pulse beats per minute)
    c. force of the beat
    d. all answers are correct

27. The balance between the heat produced and the heat lost is the _____.

    a. pulse
    b. respiration
    c. body temperature
    d. no correct answer

28. A rubber or plastic tube used to drain or inject fluid through a body opening is called _____.

    a. injection
    b. venipuncture
    c. catheter
    d. no correct answer

29. The process of inserting a catheter is called _____.

    a. major surgery
    b. catheterization
    c. specimen collection
    d. testing for venereal disease

30. When you use an autoclave, fill the water reservoir with _____.

    a. distilled water
    b. alcohol
    c. oil
    d. autoclave fluid

31. A patient positioned on her back with feet in stirrups is said to be in the _____.

    a. Sims' position
    b. sitting position
    c. lithotomy position
    d. no correct answer

32. A stethoscope is used to listen to body sounds by _____.

    a. percussion
    b. auscultation
    c. audiometry
    d. proprioceptor ideaul

33. When the physician feels with fingers or hands to determine the physical characteristics of tissues or organs it is called _____.

    a. auscultation
    b. percussion
    c. palpation
    d. measuring

34. Body temperature measured under the arm of a patient is called the _____ temperature.

    a. Oral
    b. Rectal
    c. Maxillary
    d. Axilliary

35. Listening to the sounds produced while tapping the patient with fingers is called _____.

    a. percussion
    b. audition
    c. auditive
    d. propitiation

36. The instrument used to examine the eyes is called the _____.

    a. ophthalmoscope
    b. stethoscope
    c. sphygmomanometer
    d. otoscope

37. An instrument used for auditory and sensory perception is called the _____.

    a. percussion hammer
    b. tuning fork
    c. tape measure
    d. speculum

38. An apical pulse is the method of choice for _____.

    a. infants and young children
    b. children over four years old
    c. adolescents
    d. young adults (20-40)

39. Which degree of burn is the most serious?

    a. First
    b. Second
    c. Third
    d. All answers are correct

40. On a visual acuity reading of 20/60, what does the 20 represent?

    a. Distance between patient and test chart
    b. Patient eye acuity
    c. Distance that the patient can see with glasses
    d. That the patient has perfect vision

41. Some clinical signs for head injury could be _____.

    a. vomiting
    b. headache
    c. confusion
    d. all answers are correct

42. Lying flat on one's back with arms at one's side is the _____ position.

    a. prone
    b. supine
    c. dorsal
    d. lazy

43. Lying supine with knees sharply flexed and separated is known as the _____ position.

    a. prone
    b. dorsal recumbent
    c. knee chest
    d. supine

44. When a patient's feet are placed in stirrups and the buttocks are positioned at the edge of the exam table, the patient is in the _____ position.

    a. supine
    b. prone
    c. lithotomy
    d. Sims'

45. When a patient is positioned on the abdomen, arms under the head, with the head turned to one side the patient is in the _____ position.

    a. dorsal recumbent
    b. lithotomy
    c. prone
    d. supine

46. When the patient kneels, and places his/her head and chest on the table with buttocks elevated, it is called the _____ position.

    a. knee-chest
    b. prone
    c. lithotomy
    d. proctal

47. An otoscope is used for examination of the _____.

    a. eyes
    b. ears
    c. nose
    d. mouth

48. When measuring blood pressure, the bottom number is called _____.

    a. diastolic pressure
    b. systolic pressure
    c. air pressure
    d. water pressure

49. With vital signs, any abnormal measurement must be immediately reported to the _____.

    a. patient
    b. doctor
    c. nurse
    d. orderly

50. A(n) _____ report includes information relating to the patient's main reason for scheduling an appointment to see the physician.

    a. consultation
    b. operative
    c. history and physical examination
    d. referral

V. Medical Procedures (MP)
C. Phlebotomy
and
D. Diagnostic Testing and Lab Procedures (1, 3)

Review Questions

1. The blood lancet is used for the collection of blood specimens by _____.

   a. injection
   b. suction
   c. cutting
   d. skin puncture

2. The standard point of the lancet to be used hen collecting blood from a newborn heel is _____ in length (Note: Please check current guidelines, as this changes.)

   a. 2.4 mm
   b. 3.6 mm
   c. 4.7 mm
   d. 5.5 mm

3. The most important step in the performance of a venipuncture is _____.

   a. selecting the correct needle gauge
   b. selecting the appropriate cleansing agent
   c. positively identifying the patient
   d. selecting the appropriate tourniquet

4. When cleansing the venipuncture site, it is good practice to:

   a. wipe the site back and forth quickly with an alcohol prep
   b. blow on the alcohol to dry it so it doesn't burn
   c. cleanse the site from the inside out and allow it to air dry
   d. have the patient wave the arm in the air to dry it faster

5. To determine the size of the needle remember that the higher the gauge number the _____ needle.

   a. longer
   b. smaller
   c. larger
   d. shorter

6. An instrument called a centrifuge _____.

   a. freezes specimens
   b. heats specimens
   c. is used for incubation
   d. separates the cellular and liquid portion of the blood

7. Rubber sleeves on an evacuated tube system make it possible for _____.

   a. sterilization
   b. slower draw of blood
   c. multiple use
   d. faster draw of blood

8. Preparing for a glucose tolerance test _____ hours before or during the test, the patient should not eat, smoke, drink coffee or alcohol.

   a. one
   b. ten
   c. one half
   d. two

9. In the evacuated blood collection system the evacuated glass tubes come in different sizes, and the stoppers are _____ to denote the type of additive or lack of one.

   a. striped
   b. serrated
   c. stamped
   d. color coded

10. During a venipuncture, to secure the needle during insertion into the tube stopper, you need a _____.

    a. holder
    b. sleeve
    c. tape
    d. ball of cotton

11. Which needle gauges are most commonly used for venipuncture?

    a. 24-25
    b. 21-22
    c. 19-20
    d. 16-18

12. When performing a venipuncture, the tourniquet should be wrapped around the arm about three to four inches from where you are going to _____ for a vein.

    a. apply soap
    b. scrape
    c. tap
    d. feel

13. When performing a venipuncture, if you have the patient _____ the veins will become more prominent.

    a. cough
    b. hold their breath
    c. make a fist
    d. take a deep breath

14. Which of the following is false?

    a. Veins feel like an elastic tube
    b. Veins pulsate
    c. Veins give under pressure
    d. Veins go different directions

15. Use your index finger when you _____ for a vein.

    a. stick
    b. scratch
    c. palpate
    d. inject

16. Arterioles are the smallest type of _____.

    a. tendons
    b. arteries
    c. bones
    d. veins

17. The maximum time a tourniquet should be tied on the upper arm while drawing blood is _____.

    a. 4 minutes
    b. 3 minutes
    c. 2 minutes
    d. 1 minute

18. To cleanse the typical venipuncture site, begin at the intended site of the draw and _____.

    a. work in a circle to the periphery
    b. wipe carefully back and forth
    c. cleanse vigorously for 30 seconds
    d. use a lifting motion to move away from the skin

19. The venipuncture site should be cleansed with _____.

    a. a damp solution
    b. a paper towel
    c. the back of your hand
    d. an alcohol prep

20. When using a centrifuge, make sure equal weights are _____.

    a. side by side
    b. liquid
    c. opposite each other
    d. one space apart

21. The lid to the centrifuge should be kept _____ when in use.

    a. closed
    b. open
    c. ajar
    d. lifted

22. When using an evacuated tube for collection of electrolytes use a _____.

    a. blue-top tube
    b. red-top tube
    c. black-top tube
    d. lavender-top tube

23. When collecting blood for a hematocrit test use a _____.

    a. lavender-top evacuated tube
    b. red-top evacuated tube
    c. blue-top evacuated tube
    d. yellow-top evacuated tube

24. When collecting blood for cholesterol tests use a _____ top evacuated tube.

    a. red
    b. yellow
    c. blue
    d. lavender

25. The primary anticoagulant additive EDTA removes calcium by forming insoluble or un-ionized calcium salts. It has an advantage of preventing platelet clumping and the formation of artifacts, therefore, good for the preparation of _____.

    a. background staining
    b. red cell preservation
    c. clotting
    d. blood films

26. Sodium citrate is an anticoagulant of choice for coagulation studies because it protects certain of the _____.

    a. pro-coagulants
    b. red blood cells
    c. white blood cells
    d. enzyme inhibitors

27. The tube to collect whole blood with an additive in it has a _____ stopper.

    a. red
    b. lavender
    c. green
    d. yellow

28. The color coding for a stopper of a tube with no additives is (for collection of serum) _____.

    a. green
    b. black
    c. red
    d. blue

29. At the location where you are going to feel for a vein, wrap the tourniquet around the arm approximately _____ above the area.

    a. nine to ten inches
    b. one foot
    c. three to four inches
    d. one inch

30. The cephalic, medial cubital, and basilic veins are _____ used for venipuncture.

    a. seldom
    b. never
    c. dangerous when
    d. primarily

31. When doing a venipuncture the syringe or tube should be _____ the venipuncture site to prevent back-flow.

    a. above
    b. below
    c. moved from side to side
    d. moved in and out

32. When anticoagulated blood is centrifuged _____ goes to the tope of the tube.

    a. white blood cells
    b. red blood cells
    c. plasma
    d. water

33. When anticoagulated blood is centrifuged _____ goes to the bottom of the tube.

    a. red blood cells
    b. white blood cells
    c. plasma
    d. water

34. When collecting blood by skin puncture on an infant, you should use a _____.

    a. 25 ga needle
    b. lancet
    c. scalpel
    d. 23 ga needle

35. The tube used to collect a blood sample for a Complete Blood Count (CBC) is _____.

    a. red top, no additive
    b. blue top, sodium citrate additive
    c. lavender top, ethylenediaminetetraacetic acid additive
    d. green top, lithium heparin additive

36. Which of these lab tests monitor anticoagulation therapy?

    a. PT and PTT
    b. T3 and T4
    c. Hb and Hct
    d. ABO and Rh

37. Which one of the following evacuated tubes would be drawn first?

    a. Red
    b. Lavender
    c. Gray
    d. Green

38. Making sure that a tube is correctly labeled with the patient's complete name and identification number is part of the facilities _____ plan.

    a. exposure control
    b. incident report
    c. quality control
    d. all choices

39. When performing a venipuncture if no blood flows into the tube how would you correct this situation?

    a. Gently insert the needle a little deeper
    b. Gently pull the needle out just a little
    c. Remove the needle and tourniquet and prepare another site
    d. All choices could be correct

40. If during a venipuncture a patient has a syncopal episode what would be your best course of action?

    a. Continue the draw, you need the specimen
    b. Remove the needle and tourniquet and lower the patient's head and arms
    c. Begin CPR and activate 911
    d. Restrain the patient to keep the patient from causing bodily injury

41. The most appropriate site for performing a capillary puncture in a healthy adult is the _____.

    a. great toe
    b. earlobes
    c. fingers
    d. forearms

42. It is very important when performing a capillary stick to do which one of the following?

    a. Wipe away the first drop of blood
    b. To forcefully make the puncture
    c. Not use alcohol to clean the site
    d. It is very important to do all of the above

43. Performing a _____ as part of a complete blood count determines the ratio of the volume packed red blood cells to that of whole blood.

    a. differential
    b. hematocrit
    c. hemoglobin
    d. glucose

44. _____ values are increased in infections and inflammatory disease.

   a. Glucose
   b. Hematocrit
   c. Erythrocyte sedimentation rates
   d. Coagulation studies

45. What type of blood sample will be needed to perform a hemoglobin test?

   a. EDTA added
   b. Serum only
   c. White blood cells
   d. No correct answer

46. How many hematocrit tubes should be collected from the patient?

   a. 1
   b. 2
   c. 3
   d. 5

47. What type of blood sample is needed when performing a PKU?

   a. Venipuncture
   b. Capillary
   c. Either one is acceptable
   d. No correct answer

48. A _____ is a small, sterile, needle like piece of metal used to make small punctures in the dermis.

   a. scarificator
   b. fleam
   c. lancet
   d. cup

49. In drug testing the _____ regulates describe how evidence is to be collected and handled.

   a. chain of command
   b. chain of custody
   c. person in charge
   d. local law enforcement

50. A(n) _____ requires the patient to be fasting and then blood is taken every hour for a predetermined time.

   a. cholesterol test
   b. white blood cell count
   c. differential
   d. glucose tolerance test

V. Medical Procedures (MP)
D. Diagnostic Testing and Laboratory Procedures
2. Electrocardiography

Review Questions

1. In the positioning of the electrodes, if the electrodes are placed too close together, the amplitude will be _____.

    a. small
    b. large
    c. round
    d. square

2. The large squares on the ECG paper are equal to _____.

    a. 0.10 sec
    b. 0.20 sec
    c. 0.04 sec
    d. 0.09 sec

3. A "V wave" will _____ be seen in a normal EKG.

    a. always
    b. sometimes
    c. never
    d. usually

4. The _____ switch controls the gain or amplitude on the EKG.

    a. major
    b. sensitivity
    c. red
    d. ticker

5. When preparing for lead placement you should first care for _____.

    a. skin preparation
    b. application of electrode wires
    c. application of electrodes
    d. positioning of electrodes

6. Conversion of a dysrhythmia to a normal rhythm by applying electric shock to the chest is called _____.

   a. cardiac scan
   b. pacemaker implant
   c. defibrillation
   d. endarterectomy

7. Which of the following is not a criteria for skin preparation for lead placement?

   a. Clean the skin with an alcohol swipe
   b. Make sure the skin is damp when applying the electrode
   c. Shave the hair from the skin
   d. Roughen the skin for better dermis contact

8. The electrode site should be _____.

   a. clean, smooth, and dry
   b. hairy
   c. have plenty of skin oil present
   d. moist

9. An ECG tracing measures the amount of voltage and the _____ it takes for the voltage to travel throughout the heart.

   a. time
   b. route
   c. waves
   d. lines

10. In the application of electrodes, secure the electrode by rubbing your finger around the _____ area.

    a. center
    b. gel
    c. adhesive
    d. peripheral

11. When there is no variation of R-R intervals it is called _____.

    a. irregular with a pattern
    b. absolutely regular
    c. essentially regular
    d. totally irregular

12. Ventricular depolarization produces an electrical force or vector with 2 components: (1) magnitude or force, and (2) _____.

    a. amplitude
    b. ground electrode
    c. direction or shape
    d. polarization

13. A downward or negative wave of an electrocardiogram following the P wave is the _____.

    a. R wave
    b. T wave
    c. Q wave
    d. S wave

14. A premature ventricular contraction (PVC) where the QRS have the same configuration each time they appear is called _____.

    a. uniform
    b. malignant
    c. fused
    d. bigeminy

15. When applying leads, apply the V1 lead _____.

    a. directly lateral to V4 at the anterior axillary line
    b. the fourth intercostal space right sternal border
    c. lateral to V5 at midaxillary line
    d. fifth intercostal space midclavicular line

16. Which fact is true about the P wave?

    a. Duration of the P wave is not greater than 0.11 sec
    b. Height-deflection is small, not more than 3mm
    c. Both a and b
    d. No correct answer

17. When PVC's fall on the T wave, occur in pairs, runs of 3 or more, or are multiform in nature, these conditions are called _____.

    a. Fused
    b. Multiform
    c. Life threatening
    d. Uniform

18. When a vector travels away from the positive electrode, a _____ deflection results.

    a. positive
    b. variation
    c. T wave
    d. negative

19. The combination of sensors or electrodes used for lead #1 is _____.

    a. right arm, left leg
    b. right arm, right leg
    c. left arm, right arm
    d. left arm, left leg

20. Concerning ECG's, for irregular rhythms, any method of rate calculation that depends on intervals between complexes is _____.

    a. acceptable
    b. computed using 1/2 as fast: 300/2 = 150/minute
    c. unreliable
    d. computed by counting the number of complexes in a span of 30 large boxes

21. The _____ wave represents atrial depolarization.

    a. S
    b. P
    c. R
    d. U

22. While the duration of the ST segment is not generally of clinical significance, it is an exceedingly important portion of the ECG because of _____.

    a. the fact that it follows the QRS complex
    b. shifts up or down from the baseline
    c. upward deflection from the baseline
    d. the shift away from the ischemic area

23. A QRS measurement of less than _____ seconds indicates a supraventricular pacemaker.

    a. 0.13
    b. 0.14
    c. 0.16
    d. 0.12

24. The area between waves is referred to as _____.

    a. back spaces
    b. intervals
    c. segments
    d. cycles

25. A terminal lethal dysrhythmia, a dying heart, is called _____.

    a. agonal
    b. asystole
    c. agonist
    d. agogue

26. When the heart rhythm is abnormal it is referred to as _____.

    a. patent ductus arteriosus
    b. an arrhythmia
    c. an aneurysm
    d. an embolism

27. A rapid, irregular succession of chaotic bizarre waves; wide, irregular oscillations of the baseline is called ventricular _____.

    a. fibrillation
    b. standstill
    c. tachycardia
    d. rhythm

28. The absence of one or more complete cardiac cycles where the rhythm is interrupted is referred to as _____.

    a. atrial flutter
    b. sinus arrest
    c. ventricular arrhythmia
    d. sinus wenckebach

29. A special device called a "regulator" or "flow meter" is necessary when using _____.

    a. an electric thermometer
    b. a hot pad
    c. oxygen
    d. a sphygmomanometer

30. Oxygen is administered to the patient by way of a _____.

    a. catheter
    b. cannula
    c. tent
    d. all choices

31. The clean-catch urine specimen is also called _____.

    a. clean-voided specimen
    b. 24-hr urine specimen
    c. mid-stream specimen
    d. both a and c

32. A 24-hour urine specimen should be _____.

    a. kept at body temperature
    b. left open to the air
    c. kept at room temperature
    d. chilled / refrigerated

33. The fresh-fractional urine specimen is used to test urine for _____.

    a. T.B.
    b. pneumonia
    c. sugar
    d. high blood pressure

34. Another term for acetone in the urine is _____.

    a. sugar
    b. pus
    c. ketone bodies (ketones)
    d. no correct answer

35. Which test measures both sugar and acetone in the urine?

    a. Acetest
    b. Clinitest
    c. Testape
    d. Keto-diastix

36. To help classify bacteria into two groups; gram-positive and gram-negative is a special stain called _____.

    a. glass stain
    b. gram stain
    c. germicide
    d. bacteria stain

37. When preparing a blood smear from a skin puncture you should _____ the first drop.

    a. collect
    b. use
    c. wipe away
    d. wash off

38. When you pull the second slide apart from the first slide, let them _____.

    a. stand for one hour
    b. stand for four minutes
    c. air dry
    d. blow on them to dry them

39. When preparing a blood smear, the spreader slide must be made of _____.

    a. foil
    b. steel
    c. plastic
    d. glass

40. Which of these is crucial in making a blood smear for a differential blood count?

    a. Edges should be thicker than the rest
    b. Edges should be feathered
    c. Smear must be at least 1.5 inches long
    d. Edges should be in a straight line

41. The glucose tolerance test is a _____-test

    a. saliva
    b. timed
    c. finger stick
    d. dangerous

42. While ordering procedures may vary, generally a type and RH are ordered on all pregnant women. This normally is called a _____ screen.

    a. blood
    b. serum
    c. prenatal
    d. postnatal

43. Certain types of cultures, such as deep wound cultures could contain anaerobic pathogens. Which of the following conditions is required for their growth?

    a. light and oxygen
    b. absence of oxygen
    c. light and the absence of oxygen
    d. no correct answer

44. To obtain a specimen for a throat culture the _____ must be swabbed.

    a. nasopharynx and tonsillar area
    b. back of the tongue and epiglottis
    c. under the tongue and along the gum line
    d. no correct answer

45. A CLIA waived pregnancy test is based on the detection of which one of the following?

    a. Testosterone
    b. Human chorionic gonadotropin
    c. Progesterone
    d. Estrogen

46. When performing any CLIA waived test it is important do to which one of the following?

    a. Keep all CLIA waived tests refrigerated
    b. Discard quality control kits immediately upon opening the box
    c. Perform quality control testing with every new kit and routinely thereafter
    d. All answers are correct

47. Performing routine maintenance on laboratory equipment is critical. The maintenance plan should include which one of the following?

    a. Regularly scheduled check-ups
    b. Daily examination of equipment for frayed cords or broken parts
    c. Routine cleaning of the outside of the equipment with a damp cloth
    d. All answers are correct

48. When testing for occult blood which of the following specimens would be required?

    a. Stool sample
    b. Urine
    c. Semen
    d. Blood

49. When providing a patient instructions on the collection of a sample for occult blood testing, which of the following statements is correct?

    a. Dietary modifications must occur for 48 hours prior to collection of the specimen
    b. The patient should consume 20 oz. of red meat in the four hours prior to the collection of the specimen
    c. The patient should limit dairy
    d. There are no restrictions on medications – the patient should take all medications as prescribed

50. In the medical office the most frequently performed pulmonary function test is _____.

    a. nebulization
    b. spirometry
    c. sigmoidoscopy
    d. Mantoux test

References

TITLE	AUTHOR	ISBN
MEDICAL ASSISTING: ADMINISTRATIVE & CLINICAL COMPETENCIES	KEIR	0766841464
MEDICAL ASSISTING-WORKBOOK	KEIR	0766841502
FUNDAMENTALS OF ANATOMY & PHYSIOLOGY	RIZZO	1401871887
COMPREHENSIVE MEDICAL ASSISTING	LINDH	1401881246
COMPREHENSIVE MEDICAL ASSISTING WORKBOOK	LINDH	1401881254
MEDICAL ASSISTING EXAM REVIEW	CODY	1401872301
ADMINISTRATIVE MEDICAL ASSISTING	FORDNEY	076686250X
CONTEMPORARY MEDICAL OFFICE PROCEDURES	HUMPHREY	1401863450
CONTEMPORARY MEDICAL OFFICE PROCEDURES WORKBOOK	HUMPHREY	1401870686
LAW, LIABILITY & ETHICS FOR MEDICAL OFFICE PROFESSIONALS	FLIGHT	1401840337
GETTING STARTED IN THE COMPUTERIZED MEDICAL OFFICE	CORREA	1401830382
MEDICAL MANAGER STUDENT EDITION 10.0	GARTEE	1401825745
HIPAA FOR MEDICAL OFFICE PERSONNEL	KRAGER	1401865747
MEDICAL OFFICE PRACTICE	ATKINSON	1401813984
BASIC KEYBOARDING FOR THE MEDICAL OFFICE ASSISTANT	MOSS	1401811892
DELMAR'S CLINICAL MEDICAL ASSISTING	LINDH	1401881327
CLINICAL HANDBOOK FOR THE MEDICAL OFFICE	HELLER	1401832857
VENATECH IV TRAINER	VENATECH INC	1401815804
VITAL SIGNS FOR THE MEDICAL ASSISTANT CD-ROM	DELMAR	1401871240
PRINCIPLES OF PHARMACOLOGY FOR MEDICAL ASSISTING	RICE	1401880177
BODY STRUCTURES & FUNCTIONS	SCOTT	1401809952
BODY STRUCTURES & FUNCTIONS WORKBOOK	SCOTT	1401809979
GRAMMAR & WRITING SKILLS FOR THE HEALTH PROFESSIONAL	VILLEMAIRE	0766812596
THERAPEUTIC COMMUNICATIONS FOR HEALTH PROFESSIONALS	TAMPARO	0766809218
UNDERSTANDING HEALTH INSURANCE	ROWELL	1401895956
UNDERSTANDING HEALTH INSURANCE WORKBOOK	ROWELL	140189609X
UNIFORM BILLING:GUIDE TO CLAIMS PROCESSING	RIZZO	0827382235
UNDERSTANDING MEDICAL CODING: A COMPREHENSIVE GUIDE	JOHNSON	0766801047
COMPARATIVE HEALTH INFORMATION MANAGEMENT	PEDEN	1401839487
TERMINOLOGY FOR ALLIED HEALTH PROFESSIONALS	SORMUNEN	0766862925
2005 CODING WORKBOOK FOR THE PHYSICIAN'S OFFICE	COVELL	1418015520
UNDERSTANDING HOSPITAL CODING & BILLING: A WORKTEXT	DELMAR	1401879438
GUIDE TO HEALTH INSURANCE BILLING	MOISIO	0766812073
CPT SOFTBOUND EDITION 2006	AMERICAN MEDICAL	157947697X
CPT PROFESSIONAL EDITION 2006	AMERICAN MEDICAL	1579476988
CPT EXPERT 2006	AMERICAN MEDICAL	1563376822
2005 EDUCATIONAL ICD-9-CM VOLUMES 1, 2 & 3 & HCPCS LEVEL II	INGENIX	1563299569
ICD-9-CM PROFESSIONAL FOR PHYSICIANS,VOLS 1&2-2006	INGENIX	1563376970
ICD-9-CM EXPERT FOR PHYSICIANS, VOLUMES 1 & 2-2006	INGENIX	1563376997
ICD-9-CM PROFESSIONAL FOR HOSPITALS, VOLS 1,2,3- 2006	INGENIX	1563377012
ICD-9-CM EXPERT FOR HOSPITALS, VOLS 1, 2 & 3-2006	INGENIX	1563377039
ICD-9-CM EXPERT HOME HLTH SRVC/NRSG FACILITIES/HOSPICES 2006	INGENIX	1563377063
HCPCS LEVEL II PROFESSIONAL 2006	INGENIX	1563376873
HCPCS LEVEL II EXPERT 2006	INGENIX	1563376849
MEDICAL CODING SPECIALIST'S EXAM REVIEW-PHYSICIAN	OLSEN	1401838545
MEDICAL CODING SPECIALIST'S EXAM REVIEW-HOSPITAL	OLSEN	1401837506

Title	Author	ISBN
ESSENTIALS OF HEALTH INFORMATION MANAGEMENT	GREEN	0766845028
INGENIX CODING LAB: MEDICAL BILLING BASICS 2006	INGENIX	1563377225
INGENIX CODING LAB: PHYSICIAN OFFICES 2006	INGENIX	1563377233
INGENIX CODING LAB: FACILITIES & ANCILLARY SERVICES 2006	INGENIX	1563377241
INGENIX CODING LAB: CODING FROM THE OPERATIVE REPORT 2006	INGENIX	1563377276
INGENIX CODING LAB: UNDERSTANDING E/M CODING 2006	INGENIX	1563377284
INGENIX CODING LAB: ICD-10 IMPLEMENTATION 2006	INGENIX	1563377322
INGENIX CODING LAB: UNDERSTANDING MODIFIERS 2006	INGENIX	1563377268
E/M FAST FINDER 2006	INGENIX	1563376881
INGENIX CODING LAB: MEDICAL BILLING BASICS 2006	INGENIX	1563377225
INGENIX CODING LAB: PHYSICIAN OFFICES 2006	INGENIX	1563377233
INGENIX CODING LAB: FACILITIES & ANCILLARY SERVICES 2006	INGENIX	1563377241
2006 ICD-9-CM CODE IT FAST SOFTWARE	INGENIX	1563377152
HIPAA FOR MEDICAL OFFICE PERSONNEL	KRAGER	1401865747
DRG DESK REFERENCE 2006	INGENIX	1563377195
DRG EXPERT 2006	INGENIX	1563377187
PROFESSIONAL REVIEW GUIDE FOR CCA EXAM W/INTERACTIVE CD	PRG PUBLISHING	1932152229
PROFESSIONAL REVIEW GUIDE FOR CCS EXAM W/INTERACTIVE CD	PRG PUBLISHING	1932152202
PROFESSIONAL REVIEW GDE FOR CCS-P EXAM W/INTERACTIVE CD	PRG PUBLISHING	1932152210
PROFESSIONAL REVIEW GUIDE FOR THE CHP & CHS EXAMS	PRG PUBLISHING	1932152237
PROFESSIONAL REVIEW GUIDE FOR RHIA & RHIT W/CD	PRG PUBLISHING	1932152199
PREPARATION GUIDE FOR THE RHIA & RHIT EXAMINATION	PRG PUBLISHING	1932152148
WRITING FOR THE HEALTH PROFESSIONS	TERRYBERRY	1401841929
PRACTICAL PROBLEMS IN MATH FOR HEALTH OCCUPATIONS	SIMMERS	1401840019
MATH FOR HEALTH CARE PROFESSIONALS	KENNAMER	1401858031
MATH FOR HEALTH CARE PROFESSIONALS: QUICK REVIEW	KENNAMER	1401880053
MY POCKET MENTOR: HLTH CARE PROFESSIONALS GUIDE TO SUCCESS	GAVIOLA	1401835082
QUICK REFERENCE FOR HEALTH CARE PROVIDERS	DELMAR	1401858082
HOW TO GET A JOB IN HEALTH CARE	ZEDLITZ	0766841936
DELMAR'S DRUG REFERENCE FOR HEALTH CARE PROFESSIONALS	NOBLES	076682523X
COMPREHENSIVE MEDICAL TERMINOLOGY	JONES	1401810047
MEDICAL TERMINOLOGY:PROGRAMMED SYSTEMS APPROACH	DENNERLL	1418020214
MEDICAL TERMINOLOGY FOR HEALTH PROFESSIONS	EHRLICH	1401860265
MEDICAL TERMINOLOGY: A STUDENT-CENTERED APPROACH	MOISIO	0766815226
MEDICAL TERMINOLOGY: A STUDENT-CENTERED APPROACH FLASHCARDS	MOISIO	0766815277
ESSENTIALS OF MEDICAL TERMINOLOGY	DAVIES	0766831108
MEDICAL TERMINOLOGY MADE EASY	DENNERLL	0766826732
INTRODUCTION TO MEDICAL TERMINOLOGY	EHRLICH	140181137X
QUICK REFERENCE TO MEDICAL TERMINOLOGY	DAVIES	0766840603
QUICK REFERENCE FOR HEALTH CARE PROVIDERS	DELMAR	1401858082
MERRIAM-WEBSTER'S MEDICAL DESK DICTIONARY-HARDCOVER	MERRIAM-WEBSTER	1418000574
MEDICAL TERMINOLOGY FLASH! COMPUTERIZED FLASHCARDS	DELMAR	0766843203
DELMAR LEARNING'S MEDICAL TERMINOLOGY IMAGE LIBRARY	DELMAR	1401810098
HILLCREST MEDICAL CENTER	IRELAND/NOVAK	1401841082
MEDICAL TRANSCRIPTION & TERMINOLOGY	BURNS/MALONEY	0766826929
FORREST GENERAL MED CENTER: ADV MED TRANSCRIPTION	CONERLY-STEWART	1401833489

Part III. Case Application

Case 1 – Medical Office Management – Law & Ethics

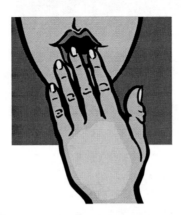

Clarissa has worked for Dr. Anne Peterson for two years. She started working in her office as a medical assistant extern. At the completion of her externship Dr. Peterson offered her the administrative medical assistant position. Clarissa enjoys her position and working for Dr. Peterson, but she is a little upset with the clinical assistant, Mallory. Mallory has worked for Dr. Peterson for six months. Clarissa has observed her making several mistakes and errors in judgment. Clarissa knows that if Dr. Peterson found out about these errors she would terminate Mallory's employment. Clarissa has known about these errors for two weeks, and ethically she is struggling with keeping quiet. Clarissa knows that Mallory is a single parent supporting two small children and she really needs this job. But just yesterday Clarissa saw Mallory helping herself to medication samples and stocking her purse with medical supplies. When Clarissa asked Mallory about it, Clarissa explained that her baby was sick and that she couldn't afford the medications. Clarissa can empathize with Mallory, but on top of yesterdays pilfering, today Clarissa received a call from the pharmacy for a prescription refill for a narcotic and the patient was Mallory. The pharmacist was concerned because the prescription had 12 refills on it and it should not have had more than one refill. This was the last straw for Clarissa.

1) What should Clarissa do? Has Mallory broken any laws. Has Clarissa?

2) What are the legal ramifications involved?

3) Were moral or ethical considerations violated? If so what are they?

Case 2 – Medical Office Management – Communication & Equipment and Supplies

Dr. Peterson has asked Clarissa to create an inventory of all of the offices administrative expendable supplies, call the suppliers to determine the most cost effective vendor, and create a document for tracking future purchases.

Create (as if you are Clarissa) the documents Dr. Peterson requested:

1. Create inventory of a minimum of 15 expendable administrative office supplies.

2. Create a written dialogue for the phone conversation between you and the vendor.

3. Design an inventory list for cost comparisons between three vendors.

4. Make up prices or use medical supply catalogs.

5. Highlight the best price for each item.

6. Create a final inventory document that can be used for future tracking purposes.

Case 3 – Medical Office Management – Financial Management

A. Dr. Peterson has seen 15 patients in the office today. Clarissa needs to file all of their charts before she leaves for the day. Put the following patients in alphabetic order by placing the numbers 1-15 on the blanks in numerical sequence with the number one being the first name and the number fifteen being the last name to be filed.

14	Sister Mary Catherine
4	William D. Fitzsimmons
5	Bill Franklin
11	Jose' Ramirez
7	Mrs. Sally Jacobson
3	Wilbur J. Fitzsimmons
12	Karenna W. Robertson
6	Bradley M. Harrison III
10	Brenda Penelope Phipps
13	Quinton Sanderson
2	Ginny Carson
9	Susanna K. Obermeister
15	Grace Wagner
1	Anastasia Anderson
8	Michaels, Amanda

B. Dr. Peterson requires all patients to pay for their charges at the time of service, with the exception of Medicare patients. Clarissa bills Medicare for these patients. Dr. Peterson expects Clarissa to collect the 20 percent that Medicare does not cover at the time of service. Grace Wagner and Wilbur J. Fitzsimmons were the only two Medicare patients Dr. Peterson treated today. The charges for Grace Wagner totaled $348.36 and the charges for Mr. Fitzsimmons totaled $96.00. How much will Clarissa need to collect from each of these patients?

C. Medicare sent an EOB for Mrs. Wagner along with a check to Dr. Peterson in the amount of $252.34. What is the balance left owing on Mrs. Wagner's account? Is Clarissa required to bill Mrs. Wagner for the balance owing, if Dr. Peterson accepts assignment?

D. You have not received an EOB or heard anything from Medicare regarding Mr. Fitzsimmons account for the past 45 days. You call Medicare and ask for the status of Mr. Fitzsimmons claim. Medicare tells you that there was an error on the claim form and you will need to correct the error and resubmit it. The diagnosis code does not support the procedure codes billed. You thank the claims' rep and located Mr. Fitzsimmon's insurance claim in your computer system. The procedure codes you submitted are listed below. For what does each procedure code stand?

99212_____

81000_____

87880_____

After review of Mr. Fitzsimmon's medical record, you realize that the diagnosis codes needed are those for Acute Pharyngitis and Urinary Frequency. What are the correct diagnosis codes?

Acute Pharyngitis_____

Urinary Frequency_____

Case 4 – Medical Terminology

Clarissa is training a new administrative medical assistant, Kyle, who graduated from a medical assistant program last year. Clarissa is very pleased with Kyle's work, but he needs help spelling medical terms and understanding all the abbreviations they use in the office. Clarissa decides that if she spends some time working with Kyle, it will save time and prevent errors. Kyle and Clarissa agree to meet after the clinic closes to review the basics of medical terminology (i.e. root words, combining vowels, prefixes and suffixes). After reviewing the basics, Clarissa will outline a plan for future review sessions. Clarissa remembers that flashcards worked well to help her review in the past, so she asks Kyle to bring a stack of 3 X 5 inch cards with him to the study sessions.

Here are some of the abbreviations giving Kyle the most trouble. See if you can identify them correctly by writing out their definitions.

bid	C	WNL
RBC	qd	ASA
GSW	stat	OS
BP	Ca	CNS
QNS	BSA	LLQ
DNA	mm	EKG
qod	Dx	cc
OU	AU	DT
STD	OTC	C&S
QC		

These are some of the root words, combining vowels, prefixes and suffixes that gave Kyle trouble. Define each term.

-itis	myelo-	-ology
kerato-	-rrhexis	cardio-
uro-	-pathy	-pexy
-stenosis	-lysis	phago-
pyo-	onycho-	-oma
heme-	bi-	tachy-
-osis	-malacia	endo-
ileo-	veni-	-rrhagia
chondro-	dys-	tracheo-
-scopy	cysto-	-rrhea
-otomy	histo-	histo-
idio-	gastro-	hystero-
-plasty	myelo-	neo-
immuno-	-ectomy	oto-

Case 5 – Anatomy & Physiology

Clarisse, Dr Peterson's Medical Assistant is reviewing Ralph Jacobson's complicated medical history. Mr. Jacobson suffers from the autoimmune disease fibromyalgia, which affects not only his muscular system but also his nervous and skeletal systems. Fibromyalgia is a very debilitating disease, affecting not only a patient physically but often the patients' mental condition. Fibromyalgia frequently causes depression due to intense constant pain and lack of normal body function.

Mr. Jacobson is also a diabetic and requires insulin injections on a daily basis. He needs to keep his insulin levels regulated so that his pancreas and kidneys keep functioning properly. Clarissa will review Mr. Jacobson's lab results for appropriate blood glucose levels. Mr. Jacobson needs to rotate his insulin injection sites daily so he does not damage his integumentary system. Clarissa will also make sure that Mr. Jacobson has regular eye exams as the fluctuation in his blood sugars can cause permanent eye damage if it goes unmonitored.

When Mr. Jacobson was diagnosed with diabetes he was scheduled to see a nutritionist. His meals need to be monitored to insure he is getting the proper nutrition and to help regulate his glucose levels. Too much or too little insulin can be fatal to someone with his condition. While having blood work drawn to monitor his diabetes and fibromyalgia, Dr Peterson discovered that Mr. Jacobson's cholesterol level was dangerously high. Dr. Peterson prescribed a statin drug to help lower his cholesterol. Clarissa will now order lipids and liver function tests on a regular basis as this medication can sometimes cause liver damage.

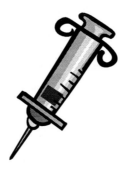

Clarissa decided she would like to learn more about both diabetes and fibromyalgia. You will be doing some of her research.

Write a brief paragraph about each of the following diseases and explain the condition and what body systems are involved.

1. Hyperlipidemia

2. Diabetes Mellitus

Case 6 – Medical Procedures – Infection and Exposure Control

Dr. Peterson has asked Clarissa to develop a written exposure control plan for their office. What items must Clarissa address?

Case 7 – Medical Procedure – Patient Examination and Clinical Skills

Case 7A. Dr. Peterson has approved Clarissa's request for two weeks of vacation, next month. She has also agreed to let Clarissa train Kyle to work as a clinical medical assistant while she is away. Clarissa decides the best way to train Kyle is to create a policy and procedure manual for the clinic. On the first day of training she has Kyle follow her around taking very thorough notes. Kyle and Clarissa will then compile the notes into an outline format for the policy and procedure manual. Their plan is to add to the outline and fill in the details as they continue Kyle's training.

Create an outline of the responsibilities associated with a clinical medical assistant in the box below.

1.
2.
3.
4.
5.
6.
7.
8.
9.
10.

Case 7B Questions

B. Kyle's first day working as a clinical assistant is one he will never forget. Kyle's first patient Mrs. Jameson came in with the chief complaint of feeling very tired and her "heart felt funny".

1. What questions should Kyle ask Mrs. Jameson?

2. What should Kyle do next?

3. What else should Kyle be thinking about doing?

4. What are Kyle's responsibilities in monitoring Mrs. Jameson?

5. In your opinion did Kyle do anything incorrectly? If so, what?

Case 8 – Medical Procedures Phlebotomy

Drawing blood was Kyle's favorite skill as a clinical medical assistant in school and he is glad that Dr. Peterson's clinic draws its own lab work rather than sending patients to an independent laboratory or draw station. Clarissa went through all of the procedures with him before she left on vacation, but did not have the opportunity to complete all the patient blood draws before she left. Dr. Peterson has ordered lab tests on Mr. Jorge and Kyle will need to draw his blood. This is his first "real" patient since his externship and he is a little nervous. Kyle looks at the lab requisition form and learns Dr. Peterson has ordered a CBC and a fasting glucose, as well as a glucose tolerance test. Kyle gathers his equipment and supplies and enters Mr. Jorge's exam room with a smile.

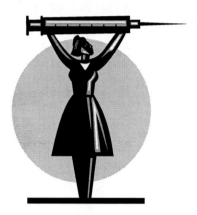

QUESTIONS for Case #8:

1. What color top tube(s) does Kyle need to draw?

2. What is the first thing Kyle should do when he enters Mr. Jorge's exam room?

3. What should Kyle do next?

4. What very important question should Kyle ask Mr. Jorge?

5. Will Kyle need to change tubes during this procedure?

6. Kyle missed Mr. Jorge's vein on the first attempt. How many times should he try before asking someone else to try?

7. After obtaining the blood specimen(s) what information should Kyle write on the tube label?

8. Are there any special circumstances Kyle will need to consider?

Case 9 – Pharmacology – Administration of Medication

The procedure Kyle has been most worried about is giving injections, especially to infants. Because Dr. Peterson is in family practice, Kyle is hoping no babies are scheduled while Clarissa is on vacation. No such luck! Dr. Peterson has asked Kyle to give Janie Hansen her MMR vaccination. Luckily Clarissa orders MMR vaccinations in pre-filled syringes and Kyle will not be required to calculate the dosages. Kyle takes Janie's chart into the exam room along with the vaccination syringe.

Questions for Case #9:

1) What should Kyle do first?

2) What should Kyle do next?

3) Provide an example of how Kyle might approach Janie to gain the best cooperation.

4) What route will Kyle use to inject the MMR vaccination?

5) Describe how best to restrain Janie.

6) Should Kyle aspirate before pushing the medication?

7) What should Kyle make sure he does before Janie and her mom leave the office?

Case 10 – Diagnostic Testing and Procedures

Clarissa is back from vacation and although Kyle enjoyed working as a clinical medical assistant he is happy to be back at the front desk, especially today. One look at the schedule and he knew Clarissa was going to be exhausted by the end of the day. Almost every one of the scheduled patient's would need diagnostic tests. Describe what each of the tests determines and/or why they would be ordered by the physician.

1. Urine HCG:

2. Rapid Strep test:

3. ESR:

4. Urinalysis:

5. Wound C&S:

6. Diff count:

7. GTT:

8. Hct:

9. Immunoassay:

10. Total cholesterol:

CONGRATULATIONS!

How did you do?

To complete your review:

(1) Look over the items you missed. If you missed several in the same topic area, you might want to refer back to your course textbook or other current reference to do some additional reading and study in that area.

(2) If the case studies were difficult for you, you may need some additional time actually performing job skills. During day to day job performance, you will come upon situations much like the cases. There will be complications and problems to solve that will draw out your critical thinking skills. This will help you with the high level questions on the actual certification examination.

(3) If you believe there might be any discrepancy in this review with current standards of practice, let us know so that we can contact the subject expert involved in this edition. Leave us a message in the "Contact Us" section of your website at www.ncctinc.com. Our phone representatives cannot answer questions about any of the content in our products. Thanks and good luck!

ANSWERS

I. Medical Office Management
A. Law and Ethics

1. c
2. a
3. c
4. d
5. b
6. b
7. c
8. b
9. b
10. c
11. b
12. c
13. c
14. a
15. c
16. d
17. b
18. c
19. d
20. b
21. b
22. a
23. c
24. a
25. d
26. c
27. c
28. b
29. a
30. b
31. a
32. a
33. b
34. b
35. b
36. b
37. a
38. b
39. c
40. c
41. d
42. a
43. a

44. a
45. b
46. b
47. a
48. b
49. c
50. c
51. b
52. b
53. b
54. c
55. a
56. c
57. d
58. c
59. d
60. d

ANSWERS

I. Medical Office Management
B. Communication, Equipment and Supplies

1. d
2. b
3. b
4. b
5. c
6. d
7. a
8. d
9. a
10. d
11. c
12. c
13. a
14. d
15. d
16. c
17. d
18. a
19. c
20. c
21. d
22. b
23. b
24. a
25. d

Answers

I. Medical Office Management
C. Financial Management

1. a
2. b
3. b
4. b
5. b
6. a
7. c
8. b
9. a
10. b
11. a
12. a
13. b
14. b
15. c
16. a
17. b
18. b
19. c
20. a
21. c
22. b
23. a
24. c
25. b
26. a
27. b
28. b
29. b
30. a
31. a
32. a
33. a
34. b
35. c
36. b
37. b
38. d
39. c
40. b
41. a
42. d
43. a
44. b

45. c
46. b
47. b
48. a
49. a
50. c

Answers

II. Medical Terminology
A. and B.

1. a
2. c
3. a
4. d
5. c
6. c
7. c
8. c
9. c
10. b
11. d
12. b
13. a
14. a
15. c
16. b
17. c
18. b
19. a
20. c
21. b
22. c
23. a
24. b
25. c
26. c
27. a
28. d
29. c
30. a
31. d
32. a
33. a
34. c
35. c
36. b

37. a
38. d
39. b
40. a
41. b
42. c
43. b
44. c
45. a
46. c
47. a
48. b
49. d
50. a
51. c
52. c
53. b
54. a
55. b
56. a
57. b
58. a
59. b
60. b
61. c
62. a
63. a

Answers

III. Pharmacology (PH)

1. b
2. b
3. a
4. a
5. c
6. a
7. b
8. a
9. b
10. a
11. b
12. b
13. b
14. b
15. b
16. c
17. a

18. b
19. c
20. a
21. a
22. a
23. b
24. c
25. a
26. a
27. a
28. b
29. a
30. a
31. b
32. d
33. b
34. a
35. b
36. a
37. a
38. a
39. b
40. d
41. c
42. d
43. c
44. a
45. a

Answers

IV. Anatomy & Physiology (AN)

1. d
2. b
3. c
4. a
5. c
6. b
7. b
8. a
9. b
10. a
11. c
12. b
13. a
14. a
15. a
16. d

17. d
18. a
19. a
20. a
21. a
22. b
23. b
24. a
25. a
26. b
27. d
28. b
29. b
30. a
31. b
32. b
33. b
34. b
35. b
36. a
37. b
38. b
39. a
40. a
41. a
42. a
43. b
44. a
45. a
46. b
47. a
48. c
49. c
50. c
51. a
52. b
53. a
54. a
55. b
56. b
57. c
58. b
59. b
60. b
61. b
62. a
63. b
64. a
65. d
66. a

67. b
68. a
69. c
70. c
71. c
72. b
73. a
74. d
75. b
76. a
77. a
78. c
79. a
80. a
81. c
82. c
83. d
84. b
85. a
86. b
87. c
88. d
89. d
90. a
91. b
92. d
93. a
94. c
95. b
96. b
97. a
98. a
99. d
100. b
101. d
102. a
103. d
104. b
105. b
106. a
107. c
108. b
109. b
110. b
111. a
112. b
113. c
114. c
115. c
116. b

117. a
118. c
119. c
120. a

Answers

V. Medical Procedures
A. Infection Control, Exposure Control, and Safety

1. a
2. a
3. c
4. c
5. a
6. b
7. c
8. d
9. b
10. c
11. a
12. d
13. a
14. c
15. b
16. c
17. d
18. b
19. c
20. a
21. b
22. b
23. d
24. b
25. a
26. b
27. b
28. a
29. b
30. c
31. c
32. d
33. b
34. d
35. a
36. a
37. c
38. b

39. b
40. c
41. d
42. b
43. d
44. c

Answers

V. Medical Procedures
B. Patient Examination and Clinical Skills

1. c
2. b
3. d
4. c
5. c
6. a
7. a
8. c
9. b
10. d
11. a
12. a
13. d
14. b
15. c
16. c
17. d
18. a
19. d
20. a
21. c
22. c
23. a
24. c
25. d
26. d
27. c
28. c
29. b
30. a
31. c
32. b
33. c
34. d
35. a
36. a
37. b

38. a
39. c
40. a
41. d
42. b
43. b
44. c
45. c
46. a
47. b
48. a
49. b
50. c

Answers

V. Medical Procedures
C. Phlebotomy And D. Diagnostic Testing (1, 3)

1. d
2. a
3. c
4. c
5. b
6. d
7. c
8. b
9. d
10. a
11. b
12. d
13. c
14. b
15. c
16. b
17. d
18. a
19. d
20. c
21. a
22. b
23. a
24. a
25. d
26. a
27. b
28. c
29. c
30. d

31. b
32. c
33. a
34. b
35. c
36. a
37. a
38. c
39. d
40. b
41. c
42. a
43. b
44. c
45. a
46. b
47. b
48. c
49. b
50. d

Answers

V. Medical Procedures
D. Diagnostic Testing and Laboratory Procedures
2. Electrocardiography

1. a
2. b
3. c
4. b
5. a
6. c
7. b
8. a
9. a
10. c
11. b
12. c
13. c
14. a
15. b
16. c
17. c
18. d
19. c

20. c
21. b
22. b
23. d
24. b
25. a
26. b
27. a
28. b
29. c
30. d
31. d
32. d
33. c
34. c
35. d
36. b
37. c
38. c
39. d
40. b
41. b
42. c
43. b
44. a
45. b
46. c
47. d
48. a
49. a
50. b

ANSWERS to Case #1: (the expert's response)

1) Clarissa should have reported the errors in judgment immediately to Dr. Peterson from the start. However now, she has no choice but to report Mallory to Dr. Peterson and to tell him the entire story, including taking the medication samples. There are serious legal and ethical implications.

2) Mallory has stolen Dr. Peterson's property and could be charged with theft. She has also committed forgery by signing Dr. Peterson's name on the prescription submitted to the pharmacy. Dr. Peterson and the pharmacy can both press charges.

3) Ethically Clarissa is as guilty as Mallory. Clarissa had a duty and a responsibility to report Mallory immediately to Dr. Peterson; in not doing so, she was (in essence) aiding and abetting Clarissa's crimes.

ANSWERS to Case #2: Answers may vary but the should contain the basic components

1. Inventory – <u>ANY</u> 15 items

    1. Printer paper
    2. Printer ink cartridges
    3. File folders
    4. File folder labels – Alphanumeric and year
    5. File folder fasteners
    6. Tape
    7. Appointment book or Appointment book pages
    8. Paper clips
    9. Staples
    10. Letterhead
    11. Envelopes
    12. Business cards
    13. Manila envelopes
    14. White-out
    15. Large binder clips
    16. Phone message pads
    17. Postage meter ink cartridges
    18. Push pins
    19. Packing tape
    20. Sticky notes

2. Vendor: Good afternoon Office Suppliers Inc. this is Jamie how may I help you today.

    Clarissa: Hello, this is Clarissa from Dr. Peterson's office. I am calling to update my expendable inventory price list. Do you have a few moments to give me some prices?

    Vendor: I would be happy to do that, Clarissa. However, do you have one of our current catalogs or have you been to our web site? All of our office supplies are listed with their prices in both places.

    Clarissa: No, I am afraid I do not have one of your catalogs, but I could go to your web site. What is your web address?

    Vendor: It is officesuppliesinc.com. If you have any questions after visiting our website please feel free to give me a call back.

    Clarissa: I will, and thank you for your time. Good-bye.

    Vendor: Good-bye.

3. & 4. & 5.

Item	Vendor #1	Vendor #2	Vendor #3
Copy paper	$27.79/case	$32.89/case	$29.49/case
Printer ink cartridges	$34.99/1	$42.00/1	$35.50/1
File folders	$5.55/100	$4.39/100	$18.05/200
File folder labels	$ 20.99/box	$34.98/box	$15.67/box
File folder fasteners	$7.78/box	$6.88/box	$5.99/box
Tape	$15.99/10 pack	$2.97 each	$5.67 2-pack
Appointment book	$30.12	$14.95	$8.60
Paper clips	$0.72/box	$1.68/box	$0.37/box
Staples	$0.94/box	$1.03/box	$0.69/box
Letterhead	$19.99/box	$23.49/box	$32.99/box
Envelopes	$4.78/box	$8.92/box	$6.65/box
Business card paper	$13.47/box	$9.47/box	$12.99/box
Manila envelops	$4.92/box	$8.93/box	$ 5.99/box
White-out	$1.88 /each	$3.48 each	$4.79/2-pack
Large binder clips	$3.12/box	$2.68/box	$1.06.box
Phone message pads	$2.25/dozen	$3.80/dozen	$2.98/dozen
Packing tape	$6.48/6-pack	$1.18/roll	$2.48/roll
Sticky notes	$6.37/5 pack	$4.63/12 pack	$8.82/dozen

6.

Item	Vendor	On-Hand	Order Quantity	Date Ordered
Copy paper	Vendor #1 $27.79/case			
Printer ink cartridges	Vendor #1 $34.99/1			
Tape	Vendor #1 $15.99/10 pack			
Letterhead	Vendor #1 $19.99/box			
Envelopes	Vendor #1 $4.78/box			
Manila envelops	Vendor #1 $4.92/box			
White-out	Vendor #1 $1.88 /each			
Phone message pads	Vendor #1 $2.25/dozen			
Packing tape	Vendor #1 $6.48/6-pack			
File folders	Vendor #2 $4.39/100			

Business card paper	Vendor #2 $13.47/box			
Sticky notes	Vendor #2 $6.37/5 pack			
File folder labels	Vendor #3 $15.67/box			
File folder fasteners	Vendor #3 $5.99/box			
Appointment book	Vendor # 3 $8.60			
Paper clips	Vendor # 3 $0.37/box			
Staples	Vendor # 3 $0.69/box			
Large binder clips	Vendor #3 $3.12/box			

ANSWERS to Case #3

A: 14, 4, 5, 11, 7, 3, 12, 6, 10, 13, 2, 9, 15, 1, 8

B. Dr. Peterson requires all patients to pay for their charges at the time of service, with the exception of Medicare patients. Clarissa bills Medicare for these patients. However Dr. Peterson expects Clarissa to collect the 20 percent Medicare does not pay at the time of service. Grace Wagner, and Wilbur J. Fitzsimmons were the only two Medicare patients Dr. Peterson treated today. The charges for Grace Wagner totaled $348.36 and the charges for Mr. Fitzsimmons totaled $96.00. How much will Clarissa collect from each of these patients?

Grace Wagner __$69.67__   Wilbur J. Fitzsimmons __$19.20__

C. Medicare sent an EOB for Mrs. Wagner along with a check to Dr. Peterson in the amount of $252.34. What is the balance left owing on Mrs. Wagner's account? __$26.35__

Is Clarissa required to bill Mrs. Wagner for the balance owed, if Dr. Peterson accepts assignment? __No__

D. Procedure Codes:

99212   Office visit, established patient, level II
81000   Urinalysis, dipstick and microscopy
87880   Strep test (CLIA – approved)

Diagnosis Codes:

Acute Pharyngitis   462
Urinary Frequency   788.41

Answers to Case #4:

Abbreviations
Bid- **twice a day**
C- **Celsius or Centigrade**
WNL- **within normal limits**
RBC- **red blood cells**
Qd- **every day**
ASA- **asprin**
GSW- **gunshot wound**
Stat- **immediately**
OS- **left eye**
BP- **blood pressure**
Ca - **Cancer**
CNS- **central nervous system**
QNS- **quantity not sufficient**
BSA- **body surface area**
LLQ- **lower left quadrant**
DNA- **deoxyribonucleic acid**
mm- **millimeter**
EKG- **electrocardiogram**
qod- **every other day**
Dx- **diagnosis**
cc- **cubic centimeters**
OU- **both eyes**
AU- **both ears**
DT- **delirium tremens**
STD- **sexually transmitted disease**
OTC- **over the counter**
C&S- **culture and sensitivity**
QC- **quality control**

Terminology
itis- **inflammation**
myelo- **spinal cord**
ology- **study**
kerato- **skin or cornea**
rrhexis- **rupture**
oto- **ear**
cardio- **heart**
uro- **urine**
pathy- **disease**
pexy- **fixation by stitching**
stenosis- **narrowing**
rrhea- **discharge**
lysis- **rupture**
phago- **eats or destroys**
pyo- **pus**
onycho- **fingernail or toenail**
oma- **tumor**
heme- **blood**
bi- **two, twice**
tachy- **rapid**
osis- **diseased, abnormal**
malacia- **softening**
endo- **inside**
ileo- **ileum**
veni- **veins**
rrhagia- **profuse flow**
chondro- **cartilage**
dys- **painful; lack of function**
tracheo- **trachea**
scopy- **inspection**
cysto- **bladder**
tomy- **cutting, incising**
histo- **tissue**
idio- **of unknown cause**
gastro- **stomach**
plasty- **repair**
thoraco- **chest**
myo- **muscle**
hystero- **uterus**
myelo- **spinal cord**
neo- **new**
immuno- **immunity**
ectomy- **remove**

ANSWERS to Case #5:

Hyperlipedemia – Is a condition involving high Cholesterol in the blood. High Cholesterol can be caused due to family history, bad diet, or a combination of both. If left undiagnosed and untreated it can lead to heart disease, blocked arteries, or death due to heart failure. There are five different levels of familial hyperlipedemia as well as three secondary hyperlipedemia levels. They have different onset factors and ages, but may still contribute to the abnormally high concentration of lipoproteins in the blood.

Diabetes – Is a general term for diseases that present with increased urination. Diabetes can affect many body systems. There are several types of diabetes, but Type 2 is the most common. It is characterized by the inability to metabolize carbohydrates, proteins and fats due to insufficient insulin production or insulin resistance. The pancreas and the Islet of Langerhans are responsible for the production of insulin that circulates in the blood system. When sugar levels in the blood become too high, glucose spills into the urine. High levels can lead to excessive thirst, one of the first symptoms of diabetes, and can result in positive glucose readings on urine dipstick tests.

ANSWERS to Case #6:

- The exposure control plan must have a timetable indicating when and how training of hazardous materials for employees will occur.

- The exposure control plan must contain a statement regarding the employer offering, at no cost to employees, hepatitis vaccination. Employees may sign a waiver if they refuse the vaccination.

- The exposure control plan must document the steps that must be taken in the event of an exposure as well as post exposure evaluation and follow up procedures.

- The exposure control plan must contain a section of implementation of engineering controls and a provision for personal protective equipment, and general housekeeping standards.

- Main areas to be covered include:
    - Personal Protective Equipment
    - Engineering Controls and Work Place Practices
    - Exposure Incident Management
    - The Right to Know Law – Material Safety Data Sheets

ANSWERS to Case #7A:

Sample Outline of Responsibilities For the Medical Assistant

- Room set up
    - Inventory and stock supplies
    - Clean room

- Patient History
    - Ask the patient question regarding their chief complaint
    - Gather subjective information and document in patient's chart

- Screening Patients
    - Gather objective information document in patient's chart
    - Vital Signs
    - Height and weight
    - Urine sample (as required)

- Patient Positioning (appropriate for type of exam)

- Assisting the physician
    - Prepare supplies and equipment (appropriate for type of exam)
    - Assist the physician as required

- Follow up care of patient

- Patient education (as appropriate)

- Order or perform lab work as required

- Clean room and prepare for next patient

ANSWERS TO CASE #7B:

Questions	Answers	Additional
1. What questions should Kyle ask Mrs. Jameson?	Kyle should ask Mrs. Jameson, ❖ How long have you felt this way? ❖ Can you describe in more detail what you mean by "Your heart feels funny"? ❖ What medications are you currently taking? ❖ Have you done anything to relieve the symptoms? ❖ Are you allergic to anything (even if her chart say she is not, it is a good idea to ask) ❖ Does anything you do make you feel better or feel worse?	Based on the responses Kyle received from Mrs. Jameson, Kyle took her vital signs (T – 99.8, P – 120 and irregular, R – 18, BP – 168/94) and then went quickly to get Dr. Peterson. Kyle was only gone for a couple of minutes locating the doctor but when he returned to Mrs. Jameson's room with Dr. Peterson, Mrs. Jameson was lying on the floor, unresponsive and bleeding from a small laceration on her forehead, apparently from the fall.
2. What should Kyle do next?	Call 911	Dr. Peterson did a quick assessment and determined that Mrs. Jameson was not breathing and did not have a pulse. Dr. Peterson asked Kyle to get the emergency crash cart, while she started CPR. Dr. Peterson asked Kyle to hook Mrs. Jameson up to the ECG machine and run a rhythm strip when he returned with the crash cart. After hooking Mrs. Jameson up to the ECG machine and running a rhythm strip Kyle looked to Dr. Peterson for his next task.
3. What else should Kyle be thinking about doing?	Kyle should think about setting up the IV equipment and starting Oxygen therapy, asking the doctor for the flow rate, or possibly seeing if Dr. Peterson wished to be relieved from performing CPR so that the IV and Oxygen and get started.	After a few minutes Dr. Peterson felt a faint pulse and shallow breath sounds. Dr. Peterson asked Kyle to monitor Mrs. Jameson while she prepared an injection and started an IV.

4. What are Kyle's responsibilities in monitoring Mrs. Jameson?	Kyle needs to monitor Mrs. Jameson's vital signs, as well as maintaining a constant observation of her ABCs. If the patient is alert, Kyle should talk to her and keep her as comfortable as possible. He could have also cleaned and bandaged Mrs. Jameson's head laceration, as needed.	While starting the IV and injecting the medication the ambulance, paramedics arrived. Kyle filled them in on everything that had happened.
5. In your opinion did Kyle do anything incorrectly? If so, what?	In my opinion, Kyle should not have left Mrs. Jameson unattended at all. To locate the doctor, he should have either used a phone (from that exam room) to page the doctor through the intercom system, or he should have watched the patient while opening the door to call for the physician outside the room.	

ANSWERS to Case #8:

1. 1 - lavender topped tube and 1 - gray topped tube

2. Identify his patient.

3. Wash his hands, put on gloves.

4. Have you been fasting for the amount of time Dr. Peterson ordered?

5. Yes

6. The rule of thumb is to try twice, and if a third attempt is required--someone else should try.

7. Patient's name, Patient's Id number (if applicable), time and date of collection, Kyle's initials.

8. Both tubes should be inverted; must draw at least ¾ of a tube of blood (no less). Mr. Jorge may need to remain in the office if a glucose tolerance test has been ordered at one hour intervals over the course of several hours, and may need to drink a measured amount of glucose after the fasting level has been drawn.

ANSWERS for Case #9:

1. Identify his patient. This is accomplished by asking the child's parent or guardian.

2. Wash his hands put on gloves (gloves are optional for injections depending on the requirements of the facility)

3. Answers will vary, but the goal is to approach Janie in a calm manner, try to make her smile, and talk to her throughout the procedure. Be proficient and efficient; do the injection right the first time. Never tell a child that it won't hurt. Even at one year old, you can explain what you are doing every step of the way. Parents or guardians are often more traumatized than the child.

4. Subcutaneous

5. It works the best if the parent or guardian will hold the child, exposing only the area for the injection. The parent can comfort the child and help keep the child distracted. If a parent or guardian is unwilling or unable to restrain the child, find another medical assistant, nurse or physician on staff who can help. Use a papoose restraint only as a last resort. Being strapped down is very traumatic for a child, and you want to give vaccinations with as little trauma as possible.

6. Yes, Kyle should aspirate, in theory. Some practices and guidelines are now recommending that aspiration is not necessary for subcutaneous injections. Kyle should follow office protocol.

7. Kyle should make friends with Janie and try to illicit a smile before they leave. Kyle should also provide Janie and her mom with information on possible reactions from the vaccination, with advice to return to the office or emergency room if any of the possible reactions should occur. Kyle should also make sure that Janie's vaccination is documented in her vaccination record.

ANSWERS for Case #10:

1. Urine HCG: Human Chorionic Gonadotropin - Pregnancy test

2. Rapid Strep test: To determine Strep throat

3. ESR: The Erythrocyte Sedimentation Rate is a screening test that confirms an inflammatory process by measuring how quickly red blood cells settle to the bottom of a calibrated tube.

4. Urinalysis: Analysis of the physical, chemical, and microscopic properties of a urine sample.

5. Wound C&S: Culture and sensitivity tests are performed to determine which antibiotic is the most effective against the cultured organism.

6. Diff count: A differential blood cell count is a test that counts the types of white blood cells in a stained blood smear while reporting cell morphology. (This is not a CLIA waived test – the medical assistant may prepare the slide but the physician or an MLT or MT must do the actual count and report)

7. GTT: Glucose Tolerance Test determines the body's ability to metabolize glucose over a specific period of time.

8. Hct: A hematocrit (HCT) is a measurement of the percentage of packed red blood cells in a volume of whole blood. A "microhematocrit" uses a very small amount of blood for the test (i.e. "micro").

9. Immunoassay: This is a laboratory technique that measures the reaction of an antigen to a specific antibody. The specimen could be collected in the office but it would then be sent to an outside lab.

10. Total cholesterol: This test would be a combination of measuring LDL and HDL cholesterol.

Please Note: The technical information in this review book was contributed by consultants who are subject matter experts in the field, but the National Center for Competency Testing does not perform any independent analysis in connection with any of the information contained herein. The NCCT Call Center staff cannot answer questions about the validity of any information contained in such review materials, as they are not subject matter experts in this field. If you have questions, please submit them to NCCT via the "contact us" function of its website www.ncctinc.com, and your questions will be forwarded to the subject matter expert(s).

NCCT does not assume, and expressly disclaims any obligation to obtain and include any information other than the information provided.